PRAISE FOR *NO REGRETS*

Dive into *No Regrets*, and discover the transformative power of commitment, hard work, and belief. A must-read for aspiring entrepreneurs!
Dr. Kathy Humel | CEO, Senior Consultant RxKHumel, LLC

If you're looking for a guide to success that's both practical and inspiring, look no further than *No Regrets* by Casel Burnett. With real-life examples and actionable advice, this book is your road map to a fulfilling and successful life.
Marshall Azar | Senior Manager, Environmental & Facilities, Toyota

Burnett's insights into the role of hard work in achieving success are both motivating and practical. A must-read for anyone serious about their goals!
Tamara Nall | CEO & Founder, The Leading Niche

Burnett's *No Regrets* is more than a book; it's a life philosophy. He shows how unwavering belief can be a driving force in achieving your dreams.
Shawn Johal | Business Growth Coach, Elevation Leaders, Bestselling Author of *The Happy Leader*

I began reading this book and couldn't put it down. Casel's life lessons are applicable to business and personal life. I learned a lot from Casel in his time at Toyota and learned more through this book. I'll be using this for my mentoring meetings moving forward.

Ryan Grimes | Senior Manager, Toyota

Having been blessed to know Casel Burnett as both a co-worker and a great friend for many years, there are many adjectives that I could use to describe him—all good. If I made myself pick one, it would be *inspirational* as from that flows many more, which only a few would be faithful, spiritual, compassionate, trustworthy, leading, wise, humorous, and instructive.

As the author of *No Regrets*, all of these adjectives could also be used to describe his book. It is a life story of Casel's journey filled with inspiration and instructions of life lessons that we all can use to be better, smarter, and more fulfilled in our own life journey so that we could at the end, as Casel will, be greeted with "Well done, faithful servant."

Paul Street | Senior Manager, TMNA (ret)

Unlock the secrets to meticulous planning and preparation with *No Regrets*. Casel Burnett lays out a blueprint for success that's both practical and inspiring.

Sanjay Jaybhay | Author of *Invest and Grow Rich*

The KEY is to "Get at it"

Life sometimes seems to be adrift as we allow analysis paralysis to creep into our thinking and ultimately our actions. *"No Regrets"* can help you re-establish a map to get going...

Are you:

- Not able to focus to determine your next steps?
- Struggling to find a way to reset?
- Feeling like you're going in circles and unable to change course?
- Wishing you could be satisfied with yourself and your work?
- Ready to try something new, but not sure where to start?

DISCOVER YOUR FREE KEYS

and begin your *"NO REGRETS"* Journey today!

NO REGRETS

WHAT MY DAD TRIED TO TEACH ME AND NOW I KNOW

CASEL BURNETT

Copyright © 2023 Casel Burnett
Published in the United States by Leaders Press.
www.leaderspress.com

All rights reserved. No part of this book may be reproduced or transmitted in any form or by any means, electronic or mechanical, including photocopying, recording, or by an information storage and retrieval system—except by a reviewer who may quote brief passages in a review to be printed in a magazine or newspaper—without permission in writing from the copyright holder.

All trademarks, service marks, trade names, product names, and logos appearing in this publication are the property of their respective owners.

ISBN 978-1-63735-240-3 (pbk)
ISBN 978-1-63735-239-7 (ebook)

Library of Congress Control Number: 2023920352

*To my dad who never wavered in his belief in me,
and I hope to do the same for my family
and friends to make a difference like he did.*

CONTENTS

Foreword xiii
Introduction 1
1. You Can Do Anything 3
2. Helping Everyone 19
3. Taking a Day Off 41
4. All of Us Believe in a Higher Power 61
5. Work Is a Part of Life, so Get Used to It 79
6. Work Never Killed Nobody 95
7. It Takes Money to Make Money 111
8. If You Keep Doing What You've Been Doing, then You'll Keep Getting What You've Been Getting 129
9. Never Stop Learning 147
10. Get at It 165
11. Closing Thoughts on the Journey 183
Casel's Bible (Created 2002) 185
A Eulogy for Casel Burnett (12/5/2016) 187
Acknowledgments 191
About Casel Burnett 193

CHAPTER 6
Work Never Killed Nobody

CHAPTER 4
All of Us Believe in a Higher Power

CHAPTER 2
Helping Everyone

CHAPTER 3
Taking a Day Off

CHAPTER 1
You Can Do Anything

CHAPTER 8
If You Keep Doing What You Been Doing, You're Going Keep Getting What You Been Getting

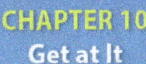
CHAPTER 10
Get at It

CHAPTER 9
Never Stop Learning

CHAPTER 7
It Takes Money to Make Money

CHAPTER 5
Work Is a Part of Life, so Get Used to It

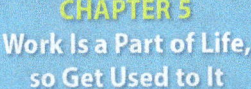

FOREWORD

No Regrets *is a life-changing reflection of Casel Burnett's journey, offering invaluable principles that guide us towards success, love, and happiness.*

—David Fernandes, president of Toyota

In *No Regrets*, Casel Burnett presents a blueprint for overcoming life's challenges that each of us encounter on this human journey. Through heartfelt storytelling, Casel shares his life lessons, encouraging readers to honor, respect, and appreciate our own experiences. By reading this book, you will embark on a personal journey, gaining profound insights that will undoubtedly shape your next chapter in life, regardless of where you currently find yourself.

The late Steve Jobs famously said, "You can't connect the dots looking forward; you can only connect them looking backward." Casel masterfully connects the dots of his own life, drawing upon his reflections to inspire readers to consider how they can connect the dots in their own upcoming chapters.

While technology continues to advance at an unprecedented pace, with companies like Amazon, Microsoft, Apple, and the recent breakthroughs in AI processes, it is crucial not to underestimate the significance of the human spirit. *No Regrets* serves as a testament to the profound impact that embracing the human spirit can have on our lives. Throughout the pages of this book, you will find numerous examples of how to infuse the human spirit into every aspect of your journey.

Allow *No Regrets* to be your guide as you embark on a transformative adventure of learning and reimagining your future. By incorporating the principles and insights shared by Casel Burnett, you will undoubtedly set yourself on the path to a successful and fulfilling future. You won't regret it!

INTRODUCTION

This book came upon me just after I had gotten over turning forty years of age. I suppose that at forty, most people start to think about their mortality: *Is my life half over?* A year before turning forty, I pondered what I had accomplished in my life thus far. I really struggled for the next year and a half asking myself, "Am I doing what God had intended me to do?"

As I had passed this crossroad in my life, I believe that some divine intervention led to several of my old friends reminding me of "Casel's Bible," which I had published in 2001 after becoming a manager in engineering (I'm attaching "Casel's Bible" here as an appendix). There it was, the note card called "Casel's Bible" that I had created to share the words and the people that had inspired me, hoping to inspire my members. It was actually still living on in the hearts of those members who were touched, which they held onto dearly in their wallets and planners.

It was that second old friend who told me, "You know, I've never forgotten what you said," and then quickly pulled that note card out of their planner that made me realize that maybe I am doing—and have been doing—what God intended me to do. It was also then that I started reflecting on even the most recent events in my life and realized that I was so very fortunate and really felt that God would say, "Well done, faithful servant."

I must note that while I was sharing the Casel's Bible events with colleagues, they suggested that I write a book. I never imagined creating a book, but I realized in 2001, when I created "Casel's Bible," that words, especially written ones, are the most powerful thing. That thought was shared by Abraham Lincoln, who helped carry our great country through its greatest trial: the Civil War. The power of the written word is ever more evident as one considers the greatest work—the Holy Bible.

YOU CAN DO ANYTHING

I remember my dad telling me in elementary school, "You can do anything you want to do if you put your mind to it." That statement came when I was at home trying to build Lincoln Logs or Legos. It also came when I was studying for school trying to win the spelling bee.

I share this first, for I now realize how this comes from the most important thing in life, which is "faith." The faith in ourselves comes from the faith that we find in God when we choose to do his will.

My father said this too as I played baseball and dreamed of hitting that home run in the crucial moment of the game. I realize now that this kept me going back into the batter's box, no matter how many times I struck out or barely got a ball in the outfield. My longest ball ever was a bouncer over the fence. That's really what faith does—it keeps our eye on the ball and keeps us going, like getting back into that batter's box.

My father was a living example as he built everything around our home. I watched him pour concrete using a wheelbarrow while building a basketball court for my brother. He used a hand-me-down basketball hoop and pole received from a neighbor who no longer had a need for it. I watched him work on our family cars while learning how to use the tools so I could fix it myself the next time. I remember helping my father put together our first shed, pouring the concrete, setting the anchors, and finally framing those walls and the roof from a kit he had bought. We later used that skill again to build his future woodshop, which was done solely from what he had put together in his mind.

I am still amazed at how my father built a carport with my brother and me, having nothing to follow but what he said. That carport fell down, hurting me and my father especially, but guess what? His faith *never* faltered. After a visit to the hospital ending in stitches in my leg to tie a major vein back together, my father, after knowing that I was okay, went right back to building that carport that evening. I remember sitting in the chaise lounge outside wishing that I could help him, for he inspired me to never give up. I now realize even more how he did so much for my faith, which was a key element in never giving up on my dreams, and that includes this book.

I remember my father lying on a cold winter's driveway as I worked on my 1967 Chevrolet pickup truck. He would just be there and occasionally ask, "Are you okay?" My dad was right there when I dropped that manual transmission on my chest and gladly helped me get it out from underneath that old Chevy pickup. My dad was right there when I sliced open my hand on the inner fender well of that old truck while I was pulling out the steering column to replace the linkage so it no longer got hung up between first and second gear, and he took me to the hospital once again to get stitches. And he was there the next day to help me finish the job.

My dad and my brother even had to put brakes on that old truck just so I could bring it home that summer just after turning fifteen years old. My dad was right there as I finished putting my first ever paint job on the body of that old truck, smiling and saying those famous words, "You can do anything you want to do if you put your mind into it." The restoration of that old truck, along with watching my dad work on our family cars, and him teaching me how to maintain them is what led to my love of automotive. That same proud feeling I had while finishing that old truck with my dad is the same feeling I have each time I accomplish something to make the next automobile at the manufacturing plants.

I remember my father teaching me how to drive a car at the age of twelve while I was delivering papers on those early Sunday mornings. He had so much faith in me that before long, he was riding in the back seat while I was driving along my paper route in our 1977 Chevrolet Caprice. The faith and trust my father had in me on those Sunday mornings led me to clean that beautiful Chevy Caprice all the time. I still remember feeling the curves in the sheet metal after I put the wax on and just enjoying the beauty of that automobile.

I remember wanting to play football at the end of my sophomore year in high school. My mom was clearly against it, and everyone warned me of the two-a-day practices, which meant I would probably get burned out and never make it to the season, for it was too much work. However, I heard those words again—"You can do anything you want to do if you put your mind to it"—which helped push me through to the season even after losing thirteen pounds on almost one-hundred-degree two-a-days. I even had to continue working in the evenings after practice so that I could put gas in that old truck.

I remember getting my first F grade in my life at Kettering University in physics class. I was so worried it might wreck my plan to transfer to the University of Dayton so I could be with my girl who's now my girl for life—my wife. Again, my dad's words rang true. My Physics 1 class at the University of Dayton was my first A-plus grade, as I lived the mindset of "You can do anything you want to do if you put your mind to it." As I dug into physics, I suddenly realized why Dad taught me the value of a "cheater bar" to break a bolt loose. It's "torque equals force times distance"—aka, a lever. I realized the scientific answer to Dad's words: "The chimney being well-built is important to the fire. Smoke rises not just because of heat, since the heated air is less dense, but also due to the change of pressure caused by the air blowing across the top of the flue since higher velocity is less pressure." All of a sudden, that kid who wanted to be an auto mechanic is sounding like an engineer and even thinking like an engineer. At that point, finishing college as an engineer was no longer a wonder but a given for Dad's words were real!

As a General Motors co-op, I found myself putting in overtime to solve equipment problems, and not the simple ones. As those evolved, I was blessed to meet and adopt Dennis Desilets as a mentor. He called me "Grasshopper." It was Dennis who took my dad's words and physics lessons to a whole new level. Dennis showed me that my dad's common sense was really true, like in trying to figure out how much pressure is needed to throw a finished seat onto a conveyor, with thoughts such as "Where do I start?" and "What does physics say about this situation?" These questions led to "torque equals force times distance," the cheater bar, or the lever. Dennis then asked me, "What's our rotation point?" realizing that this will be the distance for the seat flipper's lever arm.

By knowing the weight of the seat as the required force on the air cylinder, Dennis then asked, "What's the force on the air cylinder based on it being a circle?" If you know that the air pressure on the air cylinder is in pounds per square inch, and you know the bore or diameter, then you can calculate the area of the cylinder in square inches to get the force of the seat from the lever. Then you can estimate the needed pounds per square inch (PSI) so you can set the air cylinder to flip a seat. I now realized pumping up tires with my dad made me familiar with PSI, but now with physics, it had a whole new meaning. As I pondered the use of force from an air cylinder or an automated cheater bar, I heard Dad's words again in my head.

Just like my dad, Dennis would say, "You need any help?" It was those teacher-and-student moments that inspired me to share my life experiences and many other things I'm sharing in this book. As my experience moved on to the winter shutdowns in car plants, I started to study great automotive pioneers like Charles F. Kettering. As I was headed towards one of my first large winter shutdowns, my first daughter, Amanda, was born at Kettering Hospital, of all places. As I wandered through the hospital, I happened upon a portrait of Charles F. Kettering, with one of his personal quotes: "Nothing ever built arose to touch the skies, unless one man willed that it should; one man willed that it must."

As I pondered those words, I recalled one of Dennis's lessons: "You build things three times—once in your mind, again on paper, and finally for real." Suddenly, it came to me: "I'm going to be fine this winter shutdown, for I'm going to use my mind to build it first, and have the will of Kettering, which is *I will that it should and must.*" As I worked through the problem of rerouting the body shop conveyer with my team and studied the drawings, I remember boiling our work down to thirty-two tie-in points to be managed. I then tirelessly made an hourly based schedule so we knew when we *must* finish each tie-in, plus confirmed the order and timing necessary to meet the lead times to refill the assembly lines. As we organized the visualization of thirty-two tie-ins on the layout, with the correlation to refill the assembly line timings, I was able to use our minds to make the most precise winter shutdown plan. I remember having a final confirmation meeting with my entire team that would be covering all three shifts of work. After reviewing each of the tie-ins in detail, I closed the meeting with Kettering's quote, stating, "All of us are those who willed that it should and therefore it must." As an engineer in my twenties with a team of thirty to forty-year-olds following me and believing in the power of our minds, I realized how Charles F. Kettering, Dennis Desilets, and my dad's words truly made "real" the life lesson of "You can do anything if you put your mind to it."

We made all those thirty-two tie-ins, and I worked all night on the last day to watch all those line refills come together prior to the start-up of production at 6:30 a.m. It was awesome to see those new vehicles running from our body shop to the paint shop on a whole new path that would tie in to a new paint shop in a future phase. I remember sharing my dad's words with the plant millwrights when they wanted to do the first phase of the winter shutdown construction in-house and watching them as they embraced those first thirty-two tie-in plans as their own. I now knew how my dad's words created a bond between engineers and millwrights, which was amazing considering maintenance millwrights never cared to listen to an engineer, thinking they typically made more problems than they solved.

The success of relentless planning, reinforced by repeating Dad's "You can do anything if you put your mind to it," led to an even larger shutdown in the coming year where I tied in a whole new paint shop, eliminated an existing paint shop by a common body conveyor carrier, and added a "doors-off" build process to improve the quality of our new vehicles.

As I pondered my dad's words even more, I began to wonder what was next for my mind. At first, I just wanted to be an auto mechanic, and thanks to my mind, I was now an engineer who is now creating the ability to build new vehicles. What an amazing thought! While getting big exposure to new automobiles, my love for the automobile grew even fonder, which led me to consider "How can I share my love for cars and help others?" This thought led me to "What if I can go to the sales side of the car business?" Putting my mind to it, I began talking to my management team about my ideas, which led to an interview with the Chevrolet sales regional office in Blue Ash, Ohio.

I prepared a business plan on how to consider which cars to market and which cars needed improvements based on data. During the interview, I shared how I believed I could help them with an engineered approach to sales, and they loved the idea. I walked out of that interview thinking, *I am actually going to get to work in Chevrolet sales*. I was so excited, for my dad had raised me on Chevrolet vehicles, with my first vehicle being that 1967 Chevrolet model C10 pickup truck.

As days turned into a couple of weeks with no further follow-ups, I talked to my executive leader about the interview, who noted, "I've got you for life—newly married, a child on the way, and a house payment, which meant you're not going anywhere because you're overcommitted with family expenses." I discussed my confusion and surprise with my maintenance team members, who were twenty to thirty years older than me; they said, "You were blocked. You should call the executive at Chevrolet sales who offered you the interview." I shared that I had no idea how to get his phone number and thought who might have it, but it was most likely the executive who said, "I've got you for life."

A day later, one of my team members handed me the Chevrolet executive's name and phone number. I was so excited and nervous as I called the executive from my office desk at the General Motors Moraine plant. To my surprise, Jim answered, and he actually remembered my name and said that the Cincinnati zone office wanted to hire me. Jim shared that he had requested my resume from my executive leader but never received it. I then asked if it was okay to send it to him now and if he had a fax number, to which he then simply replied, "Sure," and gave me the fax number.

A few days later, I recognized that my maintenance team was right. I had been blocked, for my executive leader caught me in the hall with the message, "How in the _____ did you get hold of Jim? You are here for life." As my maintenance team had trained me to respond, I said, "Well, Ron, the resume I gave you for Jim must have finally reached him," which led Ron to reply, "I got you for life. You're not going anywhere." Then he stormed off. At that moment, I realized that just because your mind has a good plan, it does not mean others will let you get there. I was disappointed that my love for the automobile and Chevrolet was not going to come together at the Chevrolet zone office in Cincinnati. Putting my mind back at it led me to two different ideas:

- Mix my love of engineering with my favorite place—the world of Disney
- Continue my love for the automobile at another car maker—Toyota

My first focus was the Walt Disney Imagineering. I was fascinated by this organization, grown by Walt himself. Walt's words, "We can make your dreams come true," seemed so in line with my dad's words, "You can do anything if you put your mind to it." Hearing Walt say in his old videos, "Here at Disney, we use imagination [our minds] to turn dreams into reality," just lit me on fire for wanting to be an "Imagineer." Multiple resumes to Imagineering and a few months of silence led me to realize that my first idea was not the right one.

> **Life lesson: Putting your mind to it (a plan and actions) does not mean that it aligns with your life's (God's) purpose, so know when to adjust your mind.**

My next focus was Toyota. I remember applying to several positions. I drove to Georgetown, Kentucky, with my family just to drive by the plant. I was in awe at the size of the property and remember thinking, *I want to help Toyota give GM a run for their money*. Weeks later, I was called in for an interview at the plant. It was wonderful to talk to Bungo Hayashi, who was interviewing me for a plastics engineer job, but truly loved my experience in assembly with conveyors. The interview time quickly ran over, but once again, I felt "I am going to be an engineer at Toyota." Days later, I got a FedEx package with an offer to be an assembly engineer at Toyota in Southfield, Michigan (a Detroit suburb). As I sat there in awe of the letter, it hit me. Where better for a car lover to go than the Automobile Capital of the World, Detroit?

> **Life lesson: Putting my mind to it but adjusting the course (my goal) led to my ultimate dream— being in automotive—so life's (God's) purpose came through.**

I will never forget that last two days at General Motors, Moraine:

- Second to the last day: turning in my two-week notice on the second shift to a human resources person whom I'd never met.
- Last day: my executive leader calling me to a closed-door office with my direct supervisor, demanding to know where I'm going, clearly upset as he threw my resignation letter in response and yelling at me, "You have ten minutes to empty your desk and get out."

As I was unloading my few personal belongings at my desk, the human resources stranger from the night before was at my side with an empty box to put my belongings into. She escorted me to the turnstile, let me badge out, reconfirmed I would be getting a final paycheck, and said, "Good luck," as I headed for my car. My GM days were done for now!

Life lesson: Putting my mind to it and achieving the goal will not always align with the world's (for example, that GM executive leader's) plan for your life, so accept the difference and move on.

It's interesting that the life lesson of accepting differences from those around you would also be needed in my own family. My mother, who calls me her "Baby," has never been okay with my choice of going to Toyota due to her memories of World War II. Mom was proud of me but never had gotten comfortable enough to "trust" the Japanese until finally seeing my office in 2015, which was newly built. She said, "Wow, this is really so nice. Toyota is so good to you."

Life lesson: Putting my mind to it while accepting differences led to me learning more about my

**mother and World War II, which shows how much
we can learn on our journey to our life purpose.**

I was blessed to discover a life lesson while visiting Hiroshima on a Toyota business trip to Japan. During my Hiroshima visit, a Japanese gentleman born in 1936, which was the same year as my mom, was protesting at the last standing structure from the atomic bomb dropped on Hiroshima. He said that the Japanese government lied about the impacts of the war and the nuclear fallout and the horrific pictures of his father's melted face and his family's devastation.

Standing in downtown Hiroshima with tears streaming down my face, I realized how two completely different people, two different worlds, two different experiences (my mom hearing the cries of the families of the dead US soldiers and this man relaying the cries from the destruction and death of Japanese families) had both came to the same conclusion of "not trusting" the Japanese government.

**Life lesson: Through having new life experiences
and allowing my mind to listen to another's
perspective, I gained an even better view of the
real world and, most importantly, its people.**

As I began my Toyota career in the final assembly production engineering, I recall the rush of excitement as I walked through the parking garage in Southfield, Michigan. Now wearing a tie, dress pants, and nice leather shoes and hearing my shoes aloud in the parking, it hit me: "I hope I have a job when I get inside, for I have moved my wife and our daughter to Michigan." As I headed to the elevator of the office building, I heard my dad's words again, and my fears calmed. Walking onto the eighth floor, I saw the Toyota sign, and I let his words sink in as I listened to that first Toyota meeting.

It was fascinating to hear I was assigned to the next generation Camry, to work on the final assembly conveyors for the modification of the two Georgetown, Kentucky, plants, plus handling the ergonomic assists for the front seat install, rear seat install, instrument panel install, battery install, and a new robotic application for the spare tire install. It was comforting to be responsible for the final assembly conveyors. I quickly started gathering and organizing facts: How many conveyors and carriers are in each system? Are the investigations already done? Organizing the work was just like watching my dad rebuild the rear brakes on a vehicle by laying the parts out in the same orientation as he took them off the vehicle, for he believed in the same words of "Putting your mind to it."

As I learned the Toyota way regarding *muda*, or waste, I recognized the need to better organize my investigations at both the design center in Plymouth, Michigan, and at the manufacturing plant in Georgetown, Kentucky. Using my mind, I broke down my studies needed about the front seat installation by using cross-sections of the door opening, looking to see how many motions or postures were needed to get through the opening. I was able to determine the key points that needed checking with the real parts. Analysis in my mind allowed me to focus my time at the design center so I could efficiently use the parts, which led to both design and the Georgetown project teams trusting me to use their time, for they were interested in my organization and analysis.

Life lesson: Using my mind allowed me to capture the minds of others, leading them to want to help me and also share their ideas to improve things.

I was provided with ideas to document the "knack," which is the intuitive human process of how to maneuver the part through the door opening, like using unique part features such as targeting a corner seam to a certain place on the instrument panel at a certain angle and allowing me to establish data for each posture to ensure the most efficient and safe installation of the front seat. As I began to take my analysis of design into the manufacturing plant, I recognized the waste, or *muda*, of walking from area to area, for I had been past my next spot earlier in the day.

As I pondered eliminating the waste on my walks in the manufacturing plant, I realized that my dad taught me to not waste through the reuse of lumber, such as taking apart wood pallets to make the wood decking of my grandma Lestie's kitchen addition roof. I remember organizing the piles of wood by width and length to make sure they would line up straight and span across the joist trusses. I never recognized how much he had used his mind to build my grandmother's kitchen addition roof, for it took my dad's clear mind to build using recycled materials and know when he had gathered enough material.

Using my mind to ponder the improvements of my investigation, I had to use a gap map for the final assembly conveyors to put spaces in the line so I had room to safely investigate items. Suddenly, I realized I found the "map" I needed to organize my investigation walks at the plant.

> **Life lesson: Using my mind and realizing that I needed a map to walk by led me to find an answer by having my mind open to finding a map as I worked on other things.**

It is like buying a red car, and suddenly, you see the same car everywhere you go. It's commonly known as the "recency bias." It was so much fun to map my investigation plans, for I realized that my dad using road maps to organize our drives on family vacations was the same thing. It began to be a fun challenge to spend Monday mornings organizing my Tuesday-to-Thursday trips to the manufacturing plant in Georgetown, Kentucky.

Life lesson: Using my mind to organize my investigation led to an improvement in the on-time delivery of my bid specifications, equipment procurement, and equipment install.

Amid my successes, my manager and our team struggled to be on time with their investigations, procurement, and installation. Months into my career at Toyota, my Japanese advisor asked me, "How are you managing to stay on schedule?" I shared my weekly approach to project management with him: "Plan on Monday, investigate and gather on Tuesday to Thursday, and design and implement on Friday." Ironically, my manager was so frustrated when he was told, "You must go to the manufacturing plant five days per week," while I was able to go only two to three days per week. It came to a head in our weekly section meeting when he asked our Japanese advisor, "Why do I and my team have to go to the Georgetown plant five days per week when Casel only goes two to three days per week?" My Japanese advisor then had me share my weekly approach to project management, and only a new member shared an interest to learn my approach and use it. Even when making a weekly trip plan map became a requirement of my advisor, I watched my manager and our team just "check the box" by making one map and then complaining that it does not work, for sometimes the material or the people who have it are not there when they arrive on the map as planned.

This led to further questions by my Japanese advisor in front of the group: "What do you do, Casel, when a piece of your plan doesn't work?" I shared how I have a specific list of items for each location: "Get a drawing of this detail, measure these three or four specific details, copy these pages from the operation manual, get a picture of this view of an item so a drawing in the office makes sense, review this idea with this specific person on this detail," and so on. As I'm at each location, I check off my detail items as I complete them, plus check off or highlight each location as I complete all the items for that location.

For the next day, I then revisit the incomplete locations of my map, plus adjust the route based on what makes the most sense due to the availability of items or people needed at that location. Prior to leaving a location, I also make notes on what to look for or consider next time I'm there. It was interesting to watch the faces of my manager and team members as I shared my weekly process improvements in response to their excuses for what's not working for them—awe and silence. My Japanese advisor then explained how my approach was the ideal example of continuous improvement, which comes from the process of "plan, do, check, and act."

Life lesson: Using my mind showed me the world of continuous improvement, or kaizen, also known as the Toyota Way.

This made me realize that those same small changes or adjustments—known as baby steps to my Japanese advisors—were what allowed my dad to create amazing things like my grandma's kitchen addition, to fix brakes on his cars and others', to find wonderful spots on family vacations, and even to finish the family home that I grew up in.

It was interesting to find my dad's notes after finishing our family home in Miamisburg, Ohio: sketches with dimensions, material lists made from the sketches, and in some places, the dates were planned. At that moment. I saw the parallels between my weekly planning of my project management and my dad notetaking to finish a home. I could see that my dad lived up to his "You can do anything if you put your mind to it," for a person can create their own home for his family to grow up in, or a piece of equipment that ensures thousands of vehicles can be made, while giving livelihood to thousands of team members at the same time. Wow, Dad! What a life lesson that impacts so many people!

> **Life lesson: Using my mind to develop small improvements is how great changes seem to occur while we continue to work towards to the greater plan.**

HELPING EVERYONE

As I mentioned, my dad taught me to put my mind to it when organizing wood pallets for Grandma's kitchen. In addition, my dad put together the money to buy a house for my grandma that the kitchen addition was being put onto. This is one of my earliest memories of my dad helping everyone, for my grandma and her daughter had been asked to vacate their apartment, so they had no idea where to go. While my mom was stewing over her mom's situation, my dad just set about finding her a place to live. Interestingly enough, in all the years she lived there, my dad only charged her enough to pay the taxes. Even with no income to reinvest, he set about putting on a kitchen addition and reworking the first-floor bathroom and bedrooms so Grandma would have a living room.

My next memory is of my dad helping people at church. Joe and Freida Bussey needed a tune-up for their car, so there was my dad, in our driveway, making it happen for the cost of parts plus a modest fee for his time.

To help my brother through the low times at General Motors, my dad started "BJC Painting and Construction Maintenance." I was eleven years old, and I kept working with him until I was twenty-two. My dad's willingness to take on anything—painting three-story double houses, finishing new construction, pouring concrete sidewalks, replacing roofs, relocating walls, and repairing leaky windows, and gutters—led him to help members of our family and friends in our community. My brother struggled to continue to help him because my dad was not worried about the dollars and cents, like how much he was really making in profit after paying for his supplies, tools, gas, and wear-and-tear on his vehicle. My dad's focus was showing others he could do it as well as making things right by helping others with their project needs. If a customer felt there was any gap, whether it was something that was missed or something they did not like, then my dad would head right there to address it immediately, staying until it was right in their eyes. It was Dad's commitment to trying to make it the best that led to expanding his business by word of mouth and repeat business by satisfying his customers. I remember him getting paid to fix Aunt Hazel's porch, but only after he spent half a day clearing it off, for she loved to collect things that were piled up on the front porch. My dad didn't charge her for clearing off the porch, for that was what he did to help people.

We went to help my brother's father-in-law clear trees for a new development, and my dad's first concern was making sure he had all the wood he needed first and was completely satisfied before taking only what he needed for himself.

We helped my brother with his first home by adding a playroom with new stud walls, drywall, and the necessary electrical, which even led us to accidentally blow out the step-down transformer at the utility, but all this effort was done with no charge.

While painting in high school, my best friend needed some extra cash, so Dad added him to the payroll while showing him how to paint. My dad did the same for my childhood friend who my mom babysat so that his mother could support the family with a full-time job, and again, added him to the payroll and taught him how to paint.

My favorite memory of my dad helping everyone was regarding myself, as I wanted a car to drive when I was only fifteen years old. My first car choice was a 1967 Chevrolet C10 pickup truck that had no brakes and lots of rust. I happily paid $250, and my dad and brother helped me get it home by first putting brake shoes and the necessary brake lines on it that allowed us to just make it safe enough to drive home. My dad further helped me for weeks on end to remove the body to repair holes and put on a coat of paint. My dad never pushed his way in to help. He just stood by making sure I was okay and explained to me how to fix things that I didn't know anything about. I recall needing to replace the clutch on the manual three-speed transmission while it was cold and at night. My dad asked if I needed help, to which I replied. "I got it," but he never left my side even though I was lying on the cold ground. As the transmission finally came loose, I could not manage the weight, and it ended up falling on my chest. Now pinned under the truck with a heavy transmission on my chest, my dad asked me again, "Do you want some help?" to which I simply replied in a painful grunt, "Yes." My dad quickly grabbed the transmission and got it off me immediately, asking, "Are you all right?" I said, "I think so." My dad's only other feedback was "You better be careful."

Life lesson: True leadership is showing people the way and never abandoning them, but patiently and lovingly standing by them. It is the ultimate version of what many call today as "servant leadership."

For my dad, helping others was not a job but a commitment, an honor, and was never seen as a burden. As I further reflect on his commitment to helping others, I realize now why he had a nervous breakdown when his platoon returned from the Korean War. Most were dead, and the rest ended up in wheelchairs from injuries. It was not a nervous breakdown due to the fact of his missing a chance at death, but due to his commitment to his platoon, which he let down due to not being there to "help them." I learned of a car that Dad bought when he was reassigned to the Panama Canal build zone, rebuilt it to get it running, and then gave it to his buddy in the motor pool when he was heading back home on discharge.

My dad further showed his love for me and the community by being a Cub Scout master. At the time, he was working overtime and doing odd jobs, but he was there on Wednesday nights to lead and educate our Cub Scout pack. I remember his pride and happiness when he saw his members get through their activities to earn badges and awards. My dad would shake his members' hands with his big, calloused hands, salute them like an officer, and offer a prayer of thanks to all those attending.

Life lesson: Help not just friends and family but also those in the community. Share your pride in their accomplishments and show respect to them, to God, and to their country.

I never realized while growing up that my dad's helping others led to those passing it on by them helping the next person. In elementary school, I found myself being the chief bike mechanic for the neighborhood by pumping up tires, adjusting bicycle chains after putting them back on, and replacing tire tubes and whatever else came loose, such as seats, brakes, etc.

My learning to frame and build structures led me to volunteer to frame what was to be the new Church of the Nazarene that not only led to a place where our community would hold worship but also where I married my best friend and life partner, Michele. My dad added to my education by teaching me to help my best friends fix their cars with new floorboards, repair water pumps, tune up the motor, add on accessories, repair sheet metal, and paint the sheet metal to make it look new again.

> **Life lesson: Helping others is a way to share your knowledge and help them not only in the short term with an issue but also in the long term by giving them skills that can be used for their own livelihood as well as allowing them to pass the skill on to others, which, in short, is a true legacy.**

I never realized my dad's legacy while helping my father-in-law remodel his house until thinking about how he would comment that "Casel can do anything" and me just replying, "Thanks to my dad who taught me." I did not only help him to create a new space but also inspired him to buy more tools and gladly have him call Michele to say, "I need Casel's help when he has time."

I never realized my dad's legacy as my wife and I helped each of her sisters and brothers come into adulthood by giving them a place to stay and a vehicle to get to work. We even helped them with the purchase of cars and houses to ensure they had something for their families. Like my dad, it was not about people seeing us help others; it was doing the right thing and showing your honor to God and his people.

My learning to fix cars led me to my coworkers asking me if I could fix theirs, which now sounds familiar as I write it, because my dad did the same. I had my first opportunity when Frank, a workmate at General Motors, asked me to fix his 1970s Cadillac. The issue came from a rear-end accident. I was able to find a new bumper and taillights and straighten out the trunk line, but then I realized that the trunk pan was buckled. As always, my dad asked me, "Do you need some help?" to which I replied, "Of course," because I had no idea. I stood there in awe as I saw him gather a four-by-six-inch oak skid runner, which he laid on top of the buckle, and next came an eight-pound sledgehammer. I was amazed watching an almost sixty-year-old man, who was a farm boy, hit that oak skid runner with *kabam* and just narrowly miss the rear window frame on its way to the target. My dad never missed a stroke for over thirty minutes, working back and forth along the oak skid runner. He finally stopped, moving over the oak skid runner, felt the result, and then said, "Will that work?"

As I felt what was now barely a bump, less than a quarter of an inch, versus the almost three-inch-high mountain, I could proudly say, "Yep, I think so." As I watched my dad walk into the garage with the sledgehammer, I then tried to close the trunk lid, which had previously not worked at all. To my further astonishment, I heard the simple *click* of the trunk latch mechanism, which now was working flawlessly.

> **Life lesson: You're never too old to help, especially when you're farm-boy strong like my dad. Know that when you're willing to help, God brings others around to help you succeed.**

I truly had a moment when I realized I was dealing with a buckled floor pan and that there was no way I was fixing this one, and then up walked my dad, who used a sledgehammer with pure dead-on accuracy from his days of splitting wood on the farm in order to keep the house warm. To further recognize how fixing that Cadillac trunk pan was a miracle, I remember driving it back to work and showing Frank how good things had come out with the repair.

Frank immediately reached out his hand and said, "Great job, Casel. This is my favorite car, and my insurance company totaled it. All the shops I took it to said it could not be fixed." Frank also stood in awe as I shared how my dad helped me fix it with the thud of an eight-pound sledgehammer, replying, "Mm-hmm! That's crazy. A sledgehammer! Your dad is an awesome man."

> **Life lesson: What seems like just helping out, like my dad with that eight-pound hammer, is a miracle in the eyes of others. Thanks, Dad!**

My next adventure into helping others fix cars was buffing out the paint finish on my coworker Dan's Porsche. I was just mesmerized when I saw the Porsche sitting in my garage at the home we purchased together after getting married. Once again, my dad offered help by letting me use the same buffer that a few years before had brought out the shine on my 1967 Chevrolet pickup. As I began to work on buffing out the Porsche, I felt the body lines and was back to the days of helping my dad clean and wax the new 1977 Chevrolet Caprice. Yes, at ten years old, my dad taught me how to clean and wax a car. Now, with him teaching me to clean the paint of a car, which was helping me, and in turn, allowing me to help him, I was passing it on by helping my friend Dan clean, buff out, and wax the paint of his Porsche.

At the same time, I recalled how my brother also taught me the proper way to move the buffer in circular patterns to ensure you didn't "burn through the paint" as I first did when I was working on the 1967 Chevrolet. My brother helped his friend Rick work on cars in a body shop, so in the process, he learned how to properly care for and rehab automotive paint finishes. Once again, I realize how, when helping others, a legacy is passed through the transfer of skills.

As I began to learn more about being an engineer, Frank, who needed his Cadillac repaired, was now asking me if I could draw the plans for his new home. I hesitated at first, but Frank kept saying, "Man, I know you can do it. I saw what you did to my old Cadillac." I finally sat down with Frank, who showed me the drawings he had purchased, but now he wanted me to modify them to make the design more of a house he would want to own. It felt so special to be at a drawing board at home making new drawings like a real engineer and recalling the help I got from Mr. Bolte in seventh and eighth grade in my Industrial Arts class. I was now using those same fundamental skills to make multiple views, like top, front, right side, and isometric views. I now realized how my life in cars was turning into that engineer that Mr. McCabe at Miamisburg High School kept telling me to be. His words were, "Why work on cars as an auto mechanic when you could design and build them as an engineer?"

It was such a wonderful moment. The reason I could help Frank with his house plans as an engineer was due to Mr. McCabe helping me believe that I could be more than just an auto mechanic. Now I sit here realizing how my journey to an engineer was all due to the help of so many people:

- My dad saying, "You can do anything if you put your mind to it."
- My dad sharing his love for cars
- My dad sharing his knowledge on how to fix cars
- Mr. Bolte sharing his knowledge on how to make industrial design through drawing

- Mr. McCabe convincing me to not just be an auto mechanic

By the way, Mr. McCabe was my ninth-grade science teacher who never stopped telling me to become an engineer, even though I had signed up for joint vocational school as an auto mechanic student in the tenth grade. He then called me to the high school's principal office in tenth grade as our new assistant vice principal, asking me, "Why are you doing this? You are way smarter than this." Mr. McCabe's help in pushing me changed my life.

Life lesson: Be willing to accept help along the way, for God has a much larger purpose for us and sends his helpers at the right places and the right times.

As I reflect further on my dad's life lesson of always helping others, I now realize how much this has helped me to be a good engineer. This is the key ingredient to fix problems; it's all about our ability to help others with their issue.

My first recognition of an engineer as helping others was being asked to create a tire lift that was manually operated by a team member. In the process of studying the problem by interviewing the team member who would be using it, I heard them say, "I sure hope you can come up with a great idea because my shoulders and arms get so sore every night from having to pull on those tires to lift them up." I suddenly recognized, "Wow, I'm helping someone at work so that they can go home and enjoy their families." My work as an engineer helped them to be able to better help their family when they got home. Suddenly, my life as an engineer was more than just building a car; it was about helping the people so they can build the cars.

Life lesson: Passing on the help from others to others is key to making a difference in the world.

My initial help in the assembly plants as an engineer was mainly about helping individuals do their job more successfully. It is interesting to think how my role in developing one piece of equipment to solve a problem would lead to helping multiple individuals since that equipment was used across multiple shifts. In addition, not only did I help production team members, but I also helped maintenance team members across those multiple shifts as well. As an engineer, my output of help was multiplied, compared to serving just one customer at a time as an auto mechanic, and by accepting help to become an engineer, my ability was multiplied.

Life lesson: Be ready to accept help, knowing that your ability to help in return will be multiplied by your new abilities received from the help that was originally given to you!

As my role as an engineer developed into a project manager, I further recognized the power of help with my first conveyor project, which was called the C-to-D transfer. It moved sheet-metal-framed bodies from the C-side body shop to the D-side body shop. As I began to work on the C-to-D transfer, I was assigned an electrical engineer who focused on the controls while I focused on the mechanical design. Together, we hired an engineering firm to detail our plans so we could get the conveyor fabricated.

While studying the issues with the existing conveyor, I found that the team of maintenance folks have a wealth of knowledge on "what not to do" in the new conveyor design. Our engineering firm team also shared their dos and don'ts for conveyor design as well. As we studied the new conveyor installation, it was wonderful to have the CAD (computer-aided design) designers who could provide 3D simulations of the needed movement of the tower lifter to make sure the rigging was safe.

As we saw the impact of the existing conveyor creating major amounts of downtime, we recognized there were a few hundred people we were going to help on each shift. It was interesting to realize that with me being assigned to help fix the conveyor and by accepting help from several others that all our efforts were multiplied multiple times over. Basically, seven people were helping a few hundred people so that they would no longer have to work overtime to make the necessary parts. The help to the three hundred was multiplied by the people in their families who could now get their help since the employees would not have to work overtime.

As my responsibility grew, my next major project was building the conveyors in a new paint shop for the entire assembly plant. My help grew and doubled from seven. Our responsibility was to reroute conveyors so we could tie in to that new paint shop. I recall we were preparing for the major change to the conveyor, which had the thirty-two tie-ins mentioned earlier. The entire team of fourteen members were huddled for a week reviewing and confirming the plan.

It was a team that was going to be spread across three shifts to confirm the various tie-ins and critical individual trials to make sure the new path being changed from the first to the second floor was going to work. As I spoke to the team on that last day together, I remember being awestruck by the team helping me, for they were truly following my lead, even with a vast amount of experience of their own. I shared how important each of them was to the success of the project and how critical our success was going to be the in future of the new paint shop. That same time, we had traveled the country, with me looking for used conveyor equipment from closed facilities, which even required us to get them to certain suppliers to refurbish the components.

> **Life lesson: Let the people you help know how much you appreciate them and how their support is contributing to the greater good.**

That shutdown had some long hours and a few all-nighters for me and others, but the bond we built was amazing, along with the caring and respect we gave to each other ever since that time. Suddenly, through helping each other, I felt the closeness between us that I had felt when working on that 1967 Chevrolet pickup with my dad waiting patiently for the opportunity to offer his help. I now understand why those memories of my dad helped create a bond between us that no one could break.

That same team supported me to modify all the assembly conveyors after the new paint shop started up, including the addition of a new doors offline that allowed us to become the second plant in General Motors for such a line.

The relationship we now had from helping each other led to us challenging our new ideas, which led to some amazing innovations for the new door line. Previously, door lines were processes where doors on each side of the carrier were off-site, due to the conveyor length and location on the main conveyor line.

By properly sizing the delivery system between the locations of doors-off, we were able to keep the same sequence number of doors on the same carrier, which allowed door line members to know the model they were assembling.

Furthermore, the team that figured out the same sequence for each side of the door carrier was able to reconfigure the delivery conveyor further so that the carrier had the same vehicle, making it even better for the members to manage to build it.

Life lesson: By helping each other, we were able to innovate and improve things well beyond our individual capabilities.

My desire for working alongside others grew as we helped each other through those first few large projects. I believe these experiences led to the foundational belief of servant leadership that has been a part of my DNA as a leader. It was these experiences, plus my study and analysis of great leaders in my mastermind group, that led to one of my key thoughts, which is "Know when to lead and know when to manage."

As a person leads others, you are helping them to help themselves by reinforcing their belief in themselves. As you foster their belief in themselves, suddenly, that change in attitude towards themselves leads to a stronger inner self that allows them to help themselves. As a person managing others, your help is an external force rather than an internal one. This external force is created by the manager actually performing the help, which shows your member how much you care for and respect them as a person. When you're a manager, the external force can also be created by assigning another resource to show your member through the needed support or help, which also shows your member how much you care for and respect them as a person. My analogy for managing a member is "picking up the ball" and carrying it for them.

As I started to lead people, I realized the important lesson of helping others that my dad taught me years before through his actions with other people and myself. I realized people wanted to work for me, just like I wanted to work for my dad, and at the same time, that value of wanting to help was reciprocated as I wanted to help them too.

I found myself wanting to help them with motivation, knowledge, tools, and support to be successful. As I fostered the idea of helping them in the form of leadership versus management, I began to see the value of inner help, which allowed their abilities to suddenly multiply. I remember Tony Robbins sharing the example of "Personal Power": when a farmer learns to move dirt using a horse to pull a plow and then changes to a tractor, suddenly, the same person only doing a few acres a day is now able to do hundreds of acres a day.

As I began to consider doubling the length of lines in Princeton, Indiana, I realized I needed a way to confirm our plans since we were acting as the general contractor by hiring the individual crafts directly. Most of the organization had managed implementations or installations, but none were familiar with planning the work. To help the team, I realized we needed to "simulate" via a walk-through of our installations in each process. I organized the walk-through so that my members would explain each trade's work, with the subcontractor's leader being there as well in case there were conflicts or incomplete information. As we found struggle points and gaps, I changed the name of the walk-through to simulation, which shared the struggles we found along the way during the walk-through.

The simulation resulted in the team being able to double the length of an assembly line over a nine-day shutdown, which had not been done before and especially with folks who had never had this type of experience.

Beyond the internal team, I realized that my help in creating the simulation extended to over five hundred contractors who showed up during that nine-day winter shutdown. My help for them reciprocated to over five hundred people who are now helping over two thousand manufacturing team members to have the ability to build more products and improve their livelihood. As I reflect on this further, I realized that my team of over five hundred contractors and two thousand members had helped their own families and possibly friends with their added income, which multiplied my help in creating a simulation thousands of times over as it spread out from those impacted people.

How could I have known that the impact of one simple act, like creating a simulation, would help so many people as its effects spread across my organization and outside the organization? This idea expanded further as our team knew the challenge coming next, which was needing to rework, relocate, and install new processes to fill in that new double-length line for another 125 team-member processes.

Again, knowing our team needed a process to help them imagine "how" to implement so many process changes, I realized the answer in the word *imagine*, or visualizing in our minds, which led me to the Imagineers at Walt Disney. As I began to study how the Imagineers planned out Disney World, I realized first that they created scale models they would walk through with cameras to bring it to full lifelike scale. As I pondered this, I recognized my simulation was a full-sized walk-through model of the shutdown work.

As I further studied the Imagineer's process, I recognized another powerful tool: the Imagineers storyboard. The storyboard for the Imagineers was a series of Post-it notes with words or sketches of key milestones they wanted to have in a story, such as in a cartoon or a movie. By allowing folks to brainstorm the milestones on Post-it notes, they could just generate ideas without a need to worry about order, sequence, or timing. Once ideas were generated, they could then be moved around in a sequence or order and finally added to a timeline. Suddenly, it hit me—by helping people write storyboards for a new process, they could be engineers by solving a problem without even the need for an engineering degree.

To help my team understand storyboards, I made an example for one of our processes and a training class on the process using Microsoft Visio to make Post-it notes in digital form so that not only could we move them around but could also copy them over to use in processes that needed similar steps. As each member realized there was no wrong approach, such as the order of steps, and that they could copy and paste steps from each other, the storyboards quickly came to life.

After getting all their ideas down, I helped them put things in a logical order and finally add a timeline. From the storyboard, I helped them translate these ideas into a bid specification by having them realize that specification is like what you learned in elementary school English, which is the "5Ws and 1H": who, what, when, where, why, and how. By showing them how to use their organized storyboard in a story of 5Ws and 1H, they learned to make a bid specification. All we needed to make a bid specification complete was a layout or plan view of the process. By putting ideas into one image in order on a timeline, we not only had a layout but also one that was scalable and ideal to use for a team member process. Our team was now truly engineers, solving their problem of needing a process by simply organizing a story, then putting it into the format of a bid specification. We were able to create those 125 processes, which allowed over two thousand team members to build another model on that now double-lengthened line. Once again, just one person helping another person develop a process story led to multiplication and, eventually, the 125 processes for a new production line.

Beyond a written bid specification, those storyboards allowed us to have an order for installing the new processes. By having a timeline on the storyboard, we could then imagine a master schedule for the project. Taking the schedule and organizing things into multiple weekends where we could do the work led to our ability to create hourly schedules to manage the progress closely. Those hourly schedules helped our contractors to plan their work by organizing their labor and materials. At the end of the project, I realized how my helping a team of people to solve a problem through the simple idea of a storyboard led to new processes, doubling the length of the line and ultimately helping thousands of team members have the ability to build a new model. It is truly amazing that the impact of helping a few people solve an issue can lead to such a far reaching result.

I began to understand the value of helping many comes from the effect of helping a few. What a life lesson! I got that all from watching my dad do the same without thinking how far-reaching it would be. As I moved forward in my career, I made helping others a focal point. I expanded the idea from just tasks to bigger ideas. As my thinking matured, I realized the power of the people, and I began to not just focus on helping with individual tasks, but also on helping the people themselves.

As I finished the major shutdown, doubling the lines length, and the subsequent installation of processes, I started to realize the need for an organization or people strategy to allow us to maintain our success for the long term. Since I'd never made such a strategy before, I began studying leadership from folks like Stephen Covey, Anthony Robbins, and Napoleon Hill. My first lesson was "To begin with the end in mind," which tied back to my dad's "You can do anything if you put your mind to it." Wow, his words were ringing true again!

I realized my best way to write the end was to get at it, so I first imagined the best way for the people to be organized. At the same time, I was learning how organizations should have an operating plan that will become the set expectations and the activities to meet those expectations. With this in mind, it started to come clear to me that the people needed to be organized into two pillars called planning and implementation. Planning would allow one group of people to look ahead into the future to ensure standards were made and kept without impacting the current work being implemented; in other words, they would have the space and time to look ahead to the future with time to ponder the ideal conditions.

The implementation group would focus on how to get the work done, looking at the best materials for durability, sustainability, and efficiency, as well as labor, while thinking over the best delivery method. Delivery method allows different ways to organize the people as well, such as "Do I handle being the general contractor internally or externally, or do I give all the work to one contractor or multiple contractors?"

By considering how to organize the contractor assignments, I could help the people by managing their responsibility so that they can focus at the task at hand, creating a better product more efficiently and ultimately helping myself in the end with a clearer path to success. So helping people reciprocates in helping myself. As I finished determining the expectations for the two pillars of our organization and how to breakdown the work to our suppliers via our delivery method, I organized the necessary activities for the people into the operating plan. Once the activities were clear, I realized the need to consider which roles were required to carry out the activities. So to help my members succeed, I pondered over the skills required for each role, and I realized that training was necessary to help everyone be efficient in their work.

As we spent the next couple of years organizing our processes for planning and implementation, I watched the activities to see how effective our helping people was to the bigger picture. Interestingly, I began to realize some people thrived whether they had the necessary skills for their job or not.

As I began to study the successful people, I began to realize that individuals were successful when their character was one that was intentional: Intentional on success by being driven. Intentional on completion by having perseverance. Intentional on being driven by committing to other people and to the tasks. Intentionality led to building relationships founded on trust and maintained by the loyalty created by the continued commitment to deliver tasks to the customer or the people they were intended for.

Those who knew the skills backwards and forwards without trust and loyalty to the people were never as successful as those who had the people connection. Why? Those without the trust and loyalty of the people, whether customers or stakeholders, never received the commitment from others to go above and beyond. When my members needed an extra day to submit their requests for support in shutting down a utility or for moving existing processes to aid in construction, those who had the trust and loyalty of the people thrived while those without the people connection needed intervention or a push to get things done. Once a push was associated to an individual who was already short on the trust and loyalty of people, the gap in the relationship was further widened, creating almost a perpetual machine of declines in success no matter how capable the individual was technically.

In addition, I found myself having to use my own bank account of trust and loyalty to help those who could not get help from other people themselves. Over time, I realized that this means that I sometimes had to do extra things for people to ensure my bank account had enough room for future withdrawals. My help would not just be in the extra deliverables for a project but also in doing the simple things, such as just being a listening ear, suggesting things to help them in their own journey, making them laugh to remind them about the better side of life, or lending a hand to help them get something done for themselves.

As I reflect on helping people, I realize the power and the needs of people helping people. The power coming from the multiplication of thoughts and hands to accomplish more things in a shorter time—this has been seen over and over again as I see individual plans be turned over to an organization of people and vendors to execute it.

The need for people to have trust in each other and loyalty to each other manifest in times where projects or outcomes are struggling until one person makes a commitment to help ensure success. Once a person helps someone succeed in a task, it seems to ignite others to be driven through just one person's will of perseverance. Once success happens in one or two spots, the power of multiplication kicks in out of nowhere. What once was a disaster suddenly turns into a miracle that others then begin to want to study and talk about.

It now makes even more sense when I saw successful and happy people say, "Do you know what your dad did for me?" My dad taught me through his actions to the importance of helping others.

For myself, I heard similar words: "Do you know who taught me construction?" "Do you know who hired me as a co-op?" "Do you know who trained me as a co-op?" "Do you know who hired me full time?" It's in those moments of hearing those words that I'm the proudest of who I am for what I've been able to do for others. Through those actions, I've helped over thirty-two thousand people maintain a livelihood by building great vehicles, which then multiplies more power as they help their own families, friends, and even strangers with mobility. So, thanks, Dad for another life lesson.

TAKING A DAY OFF

Growing up with a dad who always maintained two jobs, which meant twelve-to-fifteen-hour workdays, would lead one to wonder, "Where's the work-life balance?" That same hardworking man had another side in him; a side that no one expected, especially if you worked alongside him as I did. That side was "taking a day off."

All those years, nothing had high-enough priority to overtake a Sunday. Sunday was a day to ease into—having a coffee and reading a newspaper while getting ready for church. In the summer, it was coffee on the porch and enjoying the warmth of the sunshine. In the winter, it was coffee in the recliner and enjoying the warmth of the fireplace.

My dad never mentioned the bad week at the paper mill. It was more like, "Did you hear what that crazy _____ did?" which led to a funny event at work and a hearty laugh. My dad never worried about the incomplete items of a current business job we were working on or whether he felt good or bad about our most recent work. I don't ever recall him scrambling to prepare the next day's work or even the next week's. It seemed that once we cleaned up the jobsite on Saturday evening, the job was done till Monday evening,. My dad may stay late Saturday to finish things in a good spot and put all the tools in a proper place, even when it was dark out, but then it was done.

I remember those Sundays after church. It was going to lunch at a local restaurant like Jed's Steak and Ribs, where Dad would compete with the in-laws on eating the most and/or the fastest. My brother married when I was six years old. He was thirteen years older than me, and Dad knew my brother's father-in-law from loading his truck at the docks at the paper mill. After lunch, it was family time, where I learned about the Great West, listening to the in-laws or laughing about a funny share by a family member—like my dad dumping hot coffee on himself at the dinner table, then removing the coffee-soaked garments without even thinking twice about who was at the table or even who was in the house at the same time.

I remember Sunday afternoons playing catch with a baseball in the backyard or, as I got older, a game of horseshoes. I recall stories of great baseball games my dad played in elementary school and of him and his buddies in high school playing pranks like hiding the US Post Office box. As I reflect on it now, my hardworking, driven dad made sure I knew the softer side of him—the side that was not pushing beyond physical limits in his work. It was just what my dad did on Sundays—relax and enjoy life.

As a father myself now, I realize, especially with my sons, that maybe I could have done better with that softer side. I was so proud of being a hard worker like my dad that I could not get enough of my work and assumed only good, honest people must give it all. As I would say to my sons, "Leave it all on the field." As I reflect on it now, I may have not had the sense to leave the field or take the day off. I never recognized the value of my dad's softer side until now, as I am a grandfather.

In my latest role as grandpa, I see now little men who say, "I miss my grandpa so much," "My grandpa teaches me everything," "Grandpa, I love you with all my heart," and "My grandpa is my best friend." What's so interesting is I said all those things about my dad. Whenever I thought of him, heard of him, or saw him, I had those same feelings that I now see in my grandsons toward me.

Life lesson: Stopping my life to reflect and write *No Regrets* has made me realize the value of family time especially in my latest role of grandpa.

Recently, I believe I had some heartfelt moments with my grandson, like taking a break from mowing our yard, being asked to sit down beside him in the yard, and him saying, "Grandpa, this place is beautiful." As I sat there in awe of him, I realized and told him, "Today, you taught me something. You're right, this is a beautiful place." As I sat there next to him in the yard, I recognized I had not truly sat in my own yard in the fifteen years that I owned it. Nor had I realized how beautiful our place was, especially when I saw our beautiful home in the reflection of our pond.

At the same moment, sitting with my grandson in the yard, I recalled my mom telling me fifteen years before when we were viewing the house for sale, "You always said you wanted a house on a hill with white pillars." Wow, here I was with my grandson realizing I had a lifelong dream come true. What a moment to have my three-year-old grandson show me again that taking a day off was even bigger than hanging up the boots! Taking a day off gives us that moment or space in time to realize and reflect on where you are and who you are—to be in the moment, to be thankful, and to realize the beauty of what God has put around you.

As I write in reflection, I wonder if those Sundays off were the same for my dad—a time when he could enjoy the beauty of his family and the things around him. I believe my dad knew the value of taking a day off. I never heard him complain about working too much, even though he worked six days a week, with over thirty-two years at the paper mill when he retired from there. I believe my dad knew the value of taking a day off, for I never heard him complain or even appear to worry about not getting enough done. He did leave it all on the field after sixty hours of work, but what he did better than me was to truly walk off the field, leave the stadium, to take a day off. I imagine now that he recognized the value of stopping to see how fortunate we were and how far he helped things to move and therefore improve.

> **Life lesson: Taking a day off requires not only doing your best while on the field but also knowing how to leave the field and take a break from work.**

I have read and believed Stephen Covey's "The most important time is the space between stimulus and response," which is what my dad was doing with his God, family, and friends. He was truly living in the moment or enjoying where he was and what he had accomplished. He was teaching the value of time spent with people to show his softer side, which even made me want to be closer to him and learn more from him, like my grandsons now do with their grandpa.

I hope that by better understanding taking a day off, I can stop as my dad did to enjoy my God, family, and friends, and recognize and enjoy what I have accomplished. I hope every week and, eventually, every day can be like the one where I learn, "Grandpa, you have a beautiful place," and "Grandpa, I love you with all my heart." My dad would be proud of his great-grandsons.

The other time my dad was taking a day off was on our annual summer trips to North Myrtle Beach, South Carolina. Every summer, we typically made two trips to Myrtle Beach, where we camped at the beach's travel park. I can remember my dad's happiness when he returned with warm Krispy Kreme doughnuts for breakfast. Trips with my brother's family and the in-laws were the usual. Most trips included a big family breakfast at the Aunt Jemima restaurant. Family dinners were food competitions at the K&L cafeteria or taking the big drive to Calabash, North Carolina, to eat seafood at Captain Juel's Hurricane Restaurant, where I imagined Blackbeard and a host of pirates coming in from a day at sea.

Once again, my dad unplugged from his work. I remember him jumping waves with me for what seemed like hours. Both of us would laugh and say, "Now that was a good one," when a wave got the best of us and, at times, dragged us most of the way to shore, full of water at the end. I remember him saying, "It sure is something out here," or in other words, "It's beautiful." I still was amazed to watch him carry all the beach stuff from the camper to the beach, usually a minimum of two to three loads, taking a shovel or hatchet to set the umbrella, and never even a peep of a complaint about the heat or being worn out. Taking care of things, whether at work or on vacation, was just what he did.

We always had a family trip to putt-putt golf, where my dad's pendulum-clock swing would send the ball onto a rocket launch. Even at Par 3 golf, Dad's pendulum swing at a night course led to my brother and I screaming "fore!" as the folks on the next hole ducked when they heard the whiz of the ball too.

Days at the ocean for Dad were mostly grinning and sitting under the umbrella with his Oscar cooler and a nice cold Pepsi. My dad loved to feel sand on his feet, the ocean in his ears, and the sound of the waves against the shore. In similar fashion, I found myself soaking in vacation with my family, just spending time and enjoying the moment. It is these times where I reflect on what I have done for my family, especially as I watch them and their activity during those family vacations.

It is those moments where I recognize my family's growth and maturity, which brings about the reality of progress. It is happening whether you want it to or not. I now imagine my dad pondering the same things as he sat and enjoyed his time under the umbrella. Suddenly, it makes so much sense—the pride and happiness he had for his family. He took the time on vacations to realize it.

At the same time, I can imagine him pondering the next job and being thankful for all he had accomplished. My dad started BJC Painting and Construction Maintenance so my brother would have supplemental income while starting his family. Being new at General Motors meant he could be at risk during times of layoffs. Now I can imagine that Dad must have created the idea of a painting and construction company of our own during a vacation while watching his son's family, wanting to make sure they had what they needed.

As I reflect on those trips to Myrtle Beach, I realize now how much of a stretch it was for my parents to get us there up to two times a year, but I never heard a worry or complaint about the expense. In fact, when there I remember asking to go to the waterslides and the arcade, I can't recall being told that we couldn't afford them. I was even able to take friends along as well, with no questions or comments. It seems my dad wanted us to experience the good life, and we sure did as a family. Twenty years later, I recall trying to decide whether to buy a large home and property. While standing with him on the front porch of that large home, I asked him what he thought, to which he replied, "Well, if you keep doing what you have been doing, then you'll keep getting what you have been getting." In other words, to move beyond where you are, you have to put yourself out there to change things.

I wondered how he came up with such great insight, but now I realize it was most likely what he was doing while enjoying the sound of the ocean, which was asking himself better questions. My dad has always talked of those Hillsboro, Ohio, families who had money, in his opinion, like the Larkins, Roberts, and Chambers. He would share how they had accumulated land and never had to worry about money. My dad would talk of how his dad would talk of saving money for a rainy day, so you wouldn't need to worry about it. As I have studied great thinkers like Napoleon Hill, author of *Think and Grow Rich*, I realize how he had talked of a mastermind group, taken the time to understand successful people, then pretended to be them by asking himself better questions. As I consider those things my dad talked about on those trips, I recognize he had used his study of those successful families in Hillsboro to ponder his own activity and ask himself better questions. I knew my dad and mom were considered the "lucky ones" up in Dayton, Ohio, because they took the leap of faith to move away from farming, as both their parents did, and went to the Big City.

It took not only guts and action to leave southern Ohio farming but also a vision that had to be made from looking outside where they were. As I watched Dad finish completing a home out of bankruptcy, I did not consider how much vision he must have had to finish a house started by someone else with no drawings. As years went by after trips to Myrtle Beach, suddenly, a basement bathroom came to life, plus an added driveway with a carport and a new woodshop in the backyard. All those things were built with nothing but a few sketches on a notepad and a list of materials.

I recognize that those trips to Myrtle Beach were not only to enjoy great times with his family, to show them the good life, or to show us what is beyond where you are; they were also most likely the times with himself and his mastermind group to ponder in order to create new ideas.

I wondered how he sat there under that umbrella for hours and now realize he was just enjoying his family and his life where it was now, and he must have been creating ideas for his future. I now know how much more sophisticated my dad's mind was and more so why he left the farm. My dad had a vision of his own life and was going to get at it, for he knew that if you keep doing what you have been doing, then you are going to keep getting what you have been getting. I could imagine him out in the fields on the tractor with small headlights, pondering, "This is okay, but what am I going to try next?" Mom shared that he drove the tractor all night, but now I think it was more than just getting the job done. I think my dad wanted space to think about what's next.

One of my favorite of Dad's taking-a-day-off times was our four-week trip out West. I remember the regular six- to eight-hour-per-day drives after finding a historical spot he wanted to visit, which drove my mom crazy. Our stop may be a museum, a statue, or a road sign. Once again, the camper, a Starcraft popup, was in tow behind his 1980 Chevrolet pickup truck. I remember the major storm near Wisconsin Dells, which left me sleeping in the cab of the truck with Mom and Dad in the truck topper, when a lightning bolt hit the cab. As usual, Dad checks in, "Are you okay?" and ends with a calming voice, "It will be over in the morning."

I recall the humility I felt as I stared up at Mount Rushmore. I recall the shame I felt as I saw the Native Americans on the Trail of Tears and the respect I felt as I looked at the Old West images of the Charlie Russell

Museum in Helena, Montana. I remember the wonder of the buffalo as they pushed against our truck, gently rocking it, as they crossed the road in Yellowstone National Park. I remember the cowboys singing under the stars in the KOA Campground in Jackson Hole, Wyoming, where the stars looked barely inches apart from horizon to horizon. We drove between ten-foot-high snowdrifts on the way to Crater Lake, Oregon, stopping to have a snowball fight on a day with sunny skies and seventy-degree-Fahrenheit temperatures. I remember walking into a gift shop at Crater Lake, with a guy leaning against the wall on the ground asking for me thirty-five cents for a call. I decided to ignore him, but then realized that I shouldn't. I took two steps into the door, turned around, and saw he was gone even when there was nowhere to go.

I remember pulling the popup camper across the Golden Gate Bridge and driving through downtown San Francisco with my dad just letting me go, because he trusted my driving even though I was still in high school. I remember the massiveness of the Grand Canyon in Arizona and the amazing KOA campground nearby that cooked steak dinners and had an amazing hot tub and pool.

I recognize now that the trip out West fed my lifelong desire to experience new cultures and see what great structures they built and understand their history. That trip made me realize the "Go West" mindset that fueled the US expansion of our great country. As we traveled and saw the buffalo, I could imagine being a frontiersman or a cowboy sleeping under the stars. As I studied the paintings of Charlie Russell, I could hear the Native American languages of the Indians and imagined the Indian chief's headdresses as if I had the brush in my hand painting them myself.

I remember the grandness and beauty of the trees in Yellowstone and the Grand Tetons and the amazing blue water of Crater Lake. It was the drive across Golden Gate Bridge and the busyness of downtown San Francisco that piqued my interest to experience big cities as I was discovering the latest trends in technology, fashion, and architectural design. My dad's taking the day off out West drove my desire to travel and see new lands.

> **Life lesson: By experiencing these new places and people, you are forever changed by the people, food, architecture, and history.**

I believe these new experiences help us recognize the vast size of the world God made, and the complexity of its people, their history, their homes, where they play and work. My dad had taught me that all people have a higher power that they believe in; however, they call it different things, which I can see and recognize in my travels while taking a day off. My dad himself recognized the power of life experiences, and I am forever grateful as I now reflect on my taking a day off, which has led me to learn so many wonderful things.

My favorite place for taking a day off is Walt Disney World in Florida—the place that makes my dreams come true. It's fascinating how one man who had a vision to make an amusement park where he could take his daughters created a company that has its own culture and brand. As I have visited there over the past forty years, I get more intrigued by a culture of folks dedicated to "the show," as they called it. It's amazing—the feeling of "Be our guest" that pours out from the cast members and the idea that this is the most important trip you've ever taken with your family for the first time. This atmosphere is truly why I have been back so many times. By taking a day off at Walt Disney World, I have learned and studied the

Imagineers culture of "Dream, Believe, Dare, Do," which has impacted my approach to my projects.

Another favorite place for taking a day off is the Biltmore House in Asheville, North Carolina. We now keep an annual pass for the Biltmore House so we can enjoy it as many times as we want too. What started out as the love of the estate home's size has now turned into a love of studying the details throughout the home and its property. How one man, George William Vanderbilt, could have the vision to hire enough people to make his vision come alive is amazing. George traveled globally to find the right materials and pieces for his estate home. At the same time, his grandkids saw the need to keep the vision alive and have turned it into a destination to enjoy as a guest. Biltmore also has training for those who want to learn the Biltmore way of taking care of guests, just like George and Edith Vanderbilt did themselves. I now appreciate the details of design as I build new projects across North America and pray for the vision like George had.

Taking a day off from Toyota while working in Japan led me to Kyoto, which was the original capital of Japan. I was amazed to see beautiful wooden-based structures that were thousands of years old, but they were clearly well kept and would easily last a few thousand more years. The beautiful rock gardens were perfectly manicured and were intentionally placed to create a serene view. The massiveness of the castles made with hand-hewn timbers, along with the elaborately-painted details, took my breath away. I remember being in the moment as I stared at the gold-covered exterior of the Kinkakuji Temple and the beauty of it reflecting in the perfect ponds, intentionally placed to capture its beauty.

This experience changed my views on the placement of structure, along with the simple beauty of structure combined with intentional placement of features and landscape. Beyond the placement, I realized the impact of maintenance to ensure the view was sustained, along with the fact that this contributed to its lasting thousands of years. As I enjoyed these structures with thousands of people, I was amazed how there was a reverence and respect that allowed everyone to study and just be in awe of what they saw. The Japanese have taught me the love for patience and kindness and the need to take care of things, minimize waste, respect your history, and just take baby steps every day to get better. I am forever changed by my first visit to Japan, for it made me hungry to see new countries, experience their people and culture, plus see new places to enjoy the architecture and history, learning new life lessons while taking a day off.

During one of my taking a day off days in Japan, I visited Hiroshima. I was so unsure of what to expect as an American in a place where we dropped the first atomic bomb. As I walked near the dome, which was the lone structure that survived the atomic blast, I recognized an older Japanese man who appeared to be angry. He was protesting with the pictures of his family and friends that were grossly impacted by the power and heat of the blast. As my Japanese Toyota advisor translated, I learned this man was not mad at me but at the Japanese government for lying to the people. He was born in 1936. Suddenly, I realized this Japanese man was born on the same year as my mother, who has also been mad at the Japanese for years. What an amazing parallel—my mom mad at the Japanese for the deaths of family and friends while fighting against the Japanese in a terrible war, and a Japanese man mad at the Japanese for lying about the dangers of the atomic bomb so that their people would keep fighting.

I recall standing there with tears running down my face for this man, my mom, their families, their friends, and the brave soldiers on both sides. I truly appreciated now the way two people could be mad at the same culture that I had come to love and respect as a Toyota employee.

Ironically, in another taking a day off at the Cincinnati Museum Center History section, I saw in life-size form the image of a mother crying at the front door of her home as a soldier handed her a letter of the news of her dead family member. Similarly, my mom was so deeply scarred by the war, from those screams and crying forever making her mad at the Japanese even though now they were helping me with a livelihood for me and my family.

As I wandered the museums and streets of the rebuilt Hiroshima, I stared at the historic images of a devastated people and could hear those same cries and screams that my mom could hear in a small town in Ohio happening at the same time here in a small town in Japan.

In another interesting parallel, Ohio was famous for Cincinnati Reds Baseball, and Hiroshima is famous for Reds baseball too, for they had copied our favorite pastime in Japan. I will forever remember eating lunch in a restaurant in Hiroshima, surrounded by Reds paraphernalia, reflecting on my epiphany of my mom and this Japanese man being in two different worlds but mad for the same reasons.

> **Life lesson: Experiencing cultures to learn their past, I suddenly realized that I also learned about my own cultures and my family's past.**

Now I knew why I thirsted to learn about the past, for I now understand people—that victories on one side means most likely a devastation on another side; that sometimes, whether victorious or devastated, people get seriously hurt or scarred for the same reasons; that places, whether considered good or bad, are small towns of people, whether family friends, who are just trying to enjoy life or Red's baseball. I stepped off that train as an American in a place that my country had leveled in seconds and walked back to that train station forever a changed man—a man who now better understood his mom's and a Japanese man's anger rose from a single event that forever changed the world, a man who now understood the impact of war that comes from two or more people wanting something of each other, whether it's power of control, natural resources, capital, or land. I now forever realized the power of my dad's taking a day off more than ever.

In another taking a day off in Japan, I was able to visit Tokyo where I was amazed at the power of the people, which was in stark contrast to the reverence of Kyoto or Hiroshima. In Tokyo, millions of people were always on the move on subways, trains, buses, and cars, and busily heading into skyscrapers. The lights and sounds of Tokyo were 24/7. While there, I attended a conference at the biggest expo center, most likely in the world, with an entrance just as big in height as the expo center seemed in area, across multiple floors and buildings.

At the same time of all the hustle and bustle, I could still sit down for lunch or dinner in a quiet spot where I recognized the people still enjoying each other in the midst of it all. In the hotel that evening, I sat on the balcony looking out over Tokyo, a country where millions of people were actually just living, whether in an old city of Kyoto, a rebuilt city of Hiroshima, or a forever growing city of Tokyo. They were just living to make money to support themselves and their families, just living to make a chance to have lunch or dinner with their family and friends, just living to make their voices heard so that others can learn something from their experiences, just living to experience new people and places like me who was just taking a day off. But I walked away from it forever changed in how I viewed things, and better for it.

My thirty-two trips to Japan while working for Toyota forever changed me. To be a part of a people in a place where I could not read and speak very little forced me to be in the moment to learn the power of faces and symbols and focus on the details of where I was. My dad would never have imagined his son would be learning so much from taking a day off.

Thanks to Japan and Toyota, my thirst to experience new worlds grew as we traveled to see Toyota sites in Belgium, France, and England. I will forever remember our Toyota tour guide, who spoke six languages fluently, including Polish, French, German, Japanese, and English. They were all used seamlessly whether talking to me or at the various Toyota sites he was responsible for in Europe.

While taking a day off in Brussels, I still can smell the chocolate-covered waffle and taste the chocolate-flavored Belgian beer made by the monks in the local monastery. I remember walking through the history of the city by going down through levels of archeological digs of the cobblestone streets that took me back thousands of years of Brussels history.

The details of the architecture of Brussels buildings that were well over 1,500 years old was just amazing. To see inside the Catholic churches that were built not long after Christ lived led me to a better understanding of today's altar and lector locations. These old churches had the lectors stand above the crowd in an almost-floating parapet so the crowd could hear the readings. Now that made things clearer to me why they were the way they are today, a high sacred place in the church.

I visited a flea market and found books for sale that were over 500 years old as if it was an everyday occurrence to find antiquities. I stumbled upon the famous boy peeing, which was literally on a simple street corner. I experienced a French restaurant where a local lady gladly translated the menu into English and helped us order. All that made me cherish the power of the people. My thirst to learn more about people, places, and history grew during those days in Brussels.

As a part of the Toyota trip to Europe, we finished up in London. While having a few days in the local Toyota plant, we visited the local town of Derby, where we enjoyed one of the older pubs of England, the Ye Olde Dolphin Inne, which had a stone threshold that was worn down four inches or so from almost 500 years of people walking over it. The Ye Olde Dolphin Inne led to the interest that I have in dark beers today.

Before heading back home, we ventured into downtown London. It was amazing to see the real London Bridge, the simple elegance of the Big Ben, and the local church where members of royalty have been married over the years. It was nice to use my train and subway experience from Japan to easily get around in London. The subway let us get to all key sites while enjoying dinner downtown as well. I remember sitting in an outside cafe in London and just being in awe, like, "Wow, who could have known that a Toyota career would take me to London?" While enjoying dinner with my coworkers, I was so proud and blessed by what I had been able to do. My next trip to the United Kingdom would have to include a trip to Scotland.

I was blessed to have another trip to London with a Global Logistics Conference at the local plant in Deeside. I was blessed that two of my coworkers were interested to take a trip to the Highlands of Scotland by taking a long weekend. This commitment was a big one on their part—it was an eight-hour drive from London to Edinburgh, Scotland, plus about another four hours to Aberdeen in the Highlands. I never laughed so hard in my life as when we spent multiple cycles on roundabouts, missing the appropriate exit, even though we counted with our GPS map guidance. I will always remember that first journey north to Scotland, especially when I saw the Scottish flag and the "Welcome to Scotland" sign. It felt like going home.

Our stay in Edinburgh was in an old castle turned into a Marriott hotel. We felt like kings as we enjoyed scotch and a cigar after dinner. One my friends had free drink coupons, but you had to be rooming together, to which I gladly put my arm around him and said, "We sure are" (staying together in the same room). When our third member arrived, I told him to say, "I'm staying with him," to get his free drinks, to which he was clearly not interested in saying, as we laughed and laughed.

The next morning, we headed north to Aberdeen up the coastline. It was a typical wet day in Scotland, but we didn't care, for we were on a road trip in Scotland. We first stopped at St. Andrews Golf Course and pretended to drive a golf ball off the tee near a roadside stop, plus we went to the clubhouse to get some souvenirs.

Further along the way, we stumbled onto a seaside island castle named Duntottar Castle. We had no clue until we were inside that this is where the royalty had hidden the crown jewels during a crusade. Taking a day off and being privileged to see places like St. Andrews and Duntottar made me realize that all the hard work was worth it. God had blessed us, and it even got more so as we got west of Aberdeen seeing the sign "House of Burnett." My friends were happy to say, "We made it," to me as we got out of the car at the House of Burnett parking lot.

I will never forget how special it was to have friends make sure "I made it" to the House of Burnett. They were so truly honored to help me make it there. They even put their arms around me as I stood in awe and tears at the House of Burnett. My friends said, "There it is. You made it back home." I felt such a liminal feeling as I stepped into the House of Burnett, built by my ancestors in 1536.

I felt transported back in time as I wandered through the house. I could feel my ancestors walking with me and seeing the original deed to the property just made it surreal. My friends so enjoyed my awe and excitement, which they shared on our drive back to Edinburgh. I felt such comfort there, and I felt so blessed to see a place that I had heard my dad dream about going to. I vowed to get my dad to the House of Burnett too.

Taking a day off in Edinburgh, Scotland, was such an adventure. We easily found parking while also failing to recognize the need to pay on a local parking app located on some small signs near where we parked. We visited the amazing Edinburgh castle of the famous Mary Queen of Scots and managed to shop enough that we came back to the car and dropped off our recently purchased goods.

We spent the rest of the afternoon walking around Edinburgh, and one of my coworkers wanted to drink at a local pub. I remember the crowded coziness of that local Edinburgh pub, enjoying it with my two great friends who happened to also be my coworkers. We knew it was time to head back to the hotel and enjoy some dinner since our road trip back to London the next day was going to be a long one. As we got near the spot of our rental car, I recognized the local church and the fact that our rental car was now missing.

Panic began to set in was we learned the need to pay for parking and our rental car had been towed, thanks to information provided by a local bartender working at a nearby pub who had worked for the city of Aberdeen and had towed cars to the local impound. Thanks to the help of the local bartender, we learned where the rental car was located, and he even had a friend come pick us up. The ride to the impound was stressful since my friend who had rented the car knew we needed it to get back to London the next day for our flight. We laughed as our driver got stuck in traffic. We only had seventy-five minutes before the impound closed. To add to the fun, we learned at the impound that we would need to pay about $300 each to get the car out of the impound. My friend was totally stressed out, but we gladly pitched in to pay the fine. I blocked the gate from closing since we arrived just minutes before closing while my other friend stood by the car in the impound. We were able to get the car, and it was so funny when we needed to stop for a bathroom break because our driver refused to park the car anywhere. We enjoyed those scotches that evening after dinner and could not stop laughing at our day.

Finally, years later in 2015, I was able to take my dad to Scotland to see the House of Burnett. I will never forget walking alongside my dad on the path up to the House of Burnett, saying, "There it is, Dad." We both stood there looking at the house in awe with only the sounds of him sniffling to hold back his emotions while tears of pride and joy streamed down my face. At that moment, taking a day off with my dad meant everything. I was almost fifty, helping my dad walk in his late eighties. It was like a happy ending to a life of working hard together, at first just the two of us, then Toyota keeping us at a distance for over twenty years, and had us now again taking a day off together as we did when I was little in the backyard or those summer trips to Myrtle Beach.

It was humbling to get my dad to one of his bucket-list places. I saw him struggle to get there, but I still could see that pride and happiness in his eyes. I will forever know that this was one of the last great trips with my dad, who was now struggling with age and dementia and Alzheimer's. As we drove back toward Edinburgh the next day, I realized I was blessed for taking a day off, for I almost waited too late to do so with my own dad, who had taught me such priceless lessons.

On that ride to and from the House of Burnett, I will never forget my dad being excited about those windmills and laughing as my wife would try to take pictures out the window of them, but missing her targeted image.

> **Life lesson:** That trip to Scotland to the House of Burnett with my dad really made me value the time spent with loved ones, seeing new things, learning new things, and most importantly, breathing in life, and just taking a day off. Thanks, Dad, for the life lesson.

# ALL OF US BELIEVE IN A HIGHER POWER

Growing up with my dad, we always made it to church on Sunday mornings and a lot of Sunday nights. I remember his hand going up to show the congregation, "I believe." I remember his prayer at every dinner table, "Dear Heavenly Father, thank you for bringing us together one more time. In Jesus Christ, our Savior, amen." I clearly experienced his faith in Christianity. As I began to make friends who were not only Christians but also Catholics or members of other denominations like Christian Science, etc., I started to ask my dad, "What's the difference?"

It was so interesting to hear my dad's response: "It really doesn't matter what we call him—God, Jesus, Allah, Son, Sun—for the key is that we all believe in a higher power. For no matter what people you study, they all tend to believe in a higher power." This really made so much sense to me, for clearly, there is a Mastermind or Supreme Power behind all things so we could coexist.

This has led me on such a faith-filled journey of my own. At thirteen, I remember the church summer camp where I asked for forgiveness and declared my Christianity. I was so excited to tell my brother as soon as he picked me up in his car. In college, going with my dad to a men's retreat at Higher Ground in Ohio and listening to him share of his blessings and faith in God was such a blessing to me. I watched my dad as he studied the Bible, shared his faith with me, and felt the spirit with him as we listened to the messages each night.

As I moved away from my parents, and we began a family of our own, I found myself so curious about the various types of faith, which was all based on a "higher power." As I met people that clearly seemed satisfied and happy with their life, I would find a way to learn about their journey of faith. My first memories were from a man who shared the meanings of things like Yahweh and how God was the Trinity. I had heard those words in passing in scripture but never wondered about the meaning behind them.

One of my mentors in engineering shared with me the Course in Miracles, which was a new-age faith based on God's messages today, conveyed to a person who was willing to write them down and share them. Suddenly, I was hearing God's words, like, "Do you think I'm dead? Do you think I have stopped talking to my people? Do you think all my disciples are dead, and I no longer need new ones today?" Wow, again, it made think about what I had been taught: "He is Risen." I had been taught that praying is talking to him, so why would he not want to talk to us?

As my daughter started Catholic school, I came home after my typical travels, sitting at the dinner table, praying, and then having her tell me, "I have another Father." Looking a little surprised, but not saying much other than, "Oh, you do?" I learned she was speaking of her Father in Heaven. Wow, my six-year-old daughter was now not only sharing her new faith but was also reminding me how important it was to remember my own faith. My daughter's love for her God and faith intrigued me so much that I took her and her sister to a local mass for the next several weeks. Not much later, in 2000, while in Aruba on a cruise stop point, I stumbled upon a beautiful small Catholic church along the ocean. It was full of candles. I chose to walk in with the many who were kneeling and praying, so I decided to do the same. As I prayed, suddenly, I found myself saying, "Lord, I don't know what I'm doing here, but if it's meant to be for me to be a Catholic, then give me a sign." I walked out in peace not realizing till much later it was Lent.

My sign came when a great friend at Toyota, Ron Buehler, showed up at mass, just as they were sharing about the RCIA (Rite of Christian Initiation of Adults), a process to become a member of the Catholic faith. I will never forget nervously asking Ron if he wanted to be my sponsor, to which he said, "Absolutely." What an amazing journey. The man who approved my coming to Toyota was now helping me with my faith. Ron shared his about his life growing up Catholic. He was an altar boy. He also talked about the sisters of his Catholic school and his love of the mass. Now I was learning how God's disciple Peter became the first pope of the Catholic Church when Jesus declared, "You are Peter, the Rock of my Church." Suddenly, I was realizing that one of God's disciples led the Catholic Church, which again matched my belief in the twelve disciples. I was learning from Ron that "praying is honestly a conversation with God."

Once again, my dad's thinking was right: We all believe in a "higher power." Now with Catholic faith, I learned even more clearly why the Trinity, which was the Father, Son, Holy Spirit, was so important, for there is one higher power. Similar to water, you need all three states to truly be the alpha (the beginning) and the omega (the end) as well as all that's in between. My dad's favorite hymns, like "I Saw the Light" or the "Power of Him," made more sense now than ever. As I began to learn more of how the

Catholic mass has been maintained over the years and even documented in apocalyptic code in Revelations, I realized how much more sense the Bible I read because of my dad was now making, which was followed closely in the Catholic mass and processes. I now recognized the power of being open to hear about different faiths, for now my Christian upbringing in the Nazarene Church was further reinforced and uplifted in my new journey and learnings in the Catholic faith. That newfound love of a "higher power" led me to join as a second tenor in the Cincinnati Men's Catholic Chorus. As I practiced and toured with those men, I learned more about the faith by asking about their own faith journey.

One of those men went to seminary and shared the translations of the Latin words we were singing, and once again, my faith was being strengthened as he not only shared definitions but also the origin and usage of the words in the Catholic Christian traditions. Learning Catholic really meant "universal" just made so much sense, since that is why Jesus wanted it to be the foundation of the new church based on his blood shed for us with Peter the Rock as the foundation of the church.

As we toured the Cincinnati tristate area, singing Gregorian chants and very traditional hymns, I was moved by the many people who shared the same faith and loved the traditions of the Catholic Church as I was beginning to do myself. As I sang, I found myself lifting my right hand to show my belief and realized now my dad's "higher power" was moving me. I recall moments just like him, singing with all my heart and tears streaming down my face. I never knew how important his teaching of a "higher power" was going to be in my life, but I learn more about it every day as I continue my faith journey. The Catholic or "universal" faith helped me realize even more that the "higher power" is everywhere and the signs keep on coming.

I recall my last trip in high school with my parents when we drove out West to spend four weeks going to national parks and seeing various national monuments. We were in Oregon at the Crater Lake National Park visitor center gift shop, which had an entrance that had only one way in and out. As I walked in through the gift shop screen door, a man who sat leaning against the wall asked me, "Could you loan me thirty-five cents? I need to call home?" Immediately, I said, "I don't have any change" and started to step into that gift shop. Then I realized, "It was him." I caught myself in the doorway and spun around, only to find that the man was no longer there against the wall. He was gone. For the next thirty minutes or so, I searched the entire parking lot, which was walled in by a three-foot-high stonewall, and beyond that were sheer drops from fifty to hundreds of feet below. As I walked row by row in the parking lot, I continued to watch the entrance for any type of person on foot and never saw anything even close.

As my search continued, and the minutes went by, my heart grew heavy, and my eyes filled with tears, for I knew it was him, or God putting me to the test. Worse yet, as I finally entered back into the gift shop to look for my parents, I stuck my right hand in my pocket, and sure enough, there were three dimes and a nickel. I broke into more sobbing as reality set in for thirty-five cents would not even buy one minute of a phone call. It would be long distance anywhere in 1984. Cell phones were not even a thing yet. That one event taught me the "higher power" truly existed everywhere, regardless of religion, location, race, social status, etc. My dad was right. We all believe in a "higher power," and it didn't matter what we called it or displayed it as.

From that moment on, I always feel a sixth sense when I have someone asking for help. It's like I can hear him whispering, "It's me, your Lord," as I approach them. I always get the sign in return as well as a deep stare from their eyes into mine and a "God bless you."

Immediately, my mind goes back to that 1984 video of Crater Lake playing in my head. I'm so thankful that I learned a life lesson as a young man in high school: be mindful of those in need of help, for you never know when God or that "higher power" is testing your ability to share the wonderful gifts he has already given you.

As further confirmation of my life lesson from Crater Lake, I had a similar event in the Detroit, Michigan, airport, which was even witnessed by a coworker traveling with me at the time. As I was needing to refuel the rental car before returning it, I was in the only gas station at the entrance to the airport, which is a wedge or island between the two directions of road of what is now called WG Rodell Drive. As I was sitting in the car with a coworker, I noticed a man approaching, and I heard the voice, "It's me, your Lord." Without thinking, I asked my coworker to step outside as I met up with him. The man walked up explaining that he had flown into Detroit to get back home to help his family who had just lost everything, including their home and vehicles. He was trying to gather enough money to get a taxi ride back home. He only needed thirty-seven dollars to get home and had twenty dollars already, so he would appreciate any help. I gladly gave him twenty and received the sign again of a deep stare and a "God bless you."

As my coworker started to ask me questions from outside across the car, I asked him, "Did you see where he went?" My friend and coworker immediately said, "Dude, I think he's gone. No way!" I asked him to check the parking lot and the gas station while I put up the pump and returned to my seat in the car. I smiled with amazing grace as I waited on my coworker to return from his investigation. Back in the car, he confirmed that not only was he nowhere in the parking lot, but there also is no way a pedestrian has a place to even cross the road because it was packed with moving vehicles. The road was three to four lanes wide and nonstop, so now he was wondering where he even came from. Inside the gas station, the attendant confirmed that no one was in there, including the restrooms. My coworker then exclaimed, "That guy just came in from nowhere and disappeared. It was like he was God." As we drove to turn in the rental car and rode back to the terminal in the bus, I began to explain my 1984 incident in Crater Lake to my coworker.

I realized my "higher power" had me being a witness and a disciple for the first time in my life, which made my life lesson more real than ever. It was wonderful as well to learn my coworker's belief in a higher power, for similar to my dad, he was not concerned with what a person's religion was but more about, "How can you not believe in higher power? Just look around." Only a higher power could make national treasures like the Crater Lake and the Grand Tetons. Only a higher power could create such complex things as trees, animals, etc. My dad's life lesson now made more sense as I discussed the amazing power of God with my coworker. When you consider how amazing our world is, then could there not be a higher power? As I have experienced life, the higher power has continued to provide signs and put people around me at the right times.

Growing up with my mom's mom, Grandma Lestie, I always knew she was happy and satisfied, therefore always willing to help anyone. Whether it was a place to stay, a hot meal, food from the store, or even money of her own, which was in short supply, Grandma Lestie was always willing to help. As I reflect on the experiences of a higher power, I realize now that this was most likely my Grandma Lestie teaching me her life lesson of helping others. Not long after her passing in 1997, as I was struggling with an illness during the big shutdown, doubling the size of our assembly facility, I distinctly remember a dream of her patting my cheek as she always did when I would meet her, saying "Don't worry, Casel. It will be all right." I woke up from that dream in total peace and knew Lestie is always right by me watching over me. That made her my guardian angel. In hindsight, I now realize that every time I see those strangers coming, hearing that voice, "It's me, your Lord," and doing the right thing, that Grandma Lestie is just sitting there and talking with God about how proud she is of her grandson, Casel.

My dad's life lesson of "always helping others" and "everyone believes in a higher power" now appear to reciprocate each other.

Life lesson: As we appreciate and understand a higher power, we then recognize the need to help others, for we are actually taking care of God himself.

In retrospect, as we are helping others, we learn of the higher power recognizing again that religion, location, ethnicity, social status, or anything else does not keep God or the higher power from manifesting before us if we pay attention to the signs that are always there.

As I have learned that the higher power is all around us, in the people we meet and that they help God to give us the signs we need, I will never forget the strongest and clearest sign from the higher power than when we were on our twentieth wedding anniversary in Aruba on Eagle Beach. By the way, I should have known this would be the place for a few reasons: Aruba in 2000 was where God led me to the Catholic Church, and Eagle Beach since my favorite animal is the eagle.

The trip to Aruba in 2009 was not only to celebrate our twentieth anniversary but also a chance for us to really discuss a big step that was getting ready to happen that we had not expected: the addition of two sons into our life so we could officially be a family with four kids. Unfortunately, the boys' birth father had progressed from marijuana to heroine to meth, and now it seemed that was not enough. We really wanted to make the right decision for those two little men but also realized the challenge, for the birth father was a family member. This would mean having to separate from our extended family to ensure the boys had a clean break from their difficult start in life that was no fault of their own.

As we were enjoying the sunset on Eagle Beach, my wife was walking along the water, and I was sitting in a lounge chair. As she was walking toward me, a man seemed to appear from nowhere, yelling at her while and pointing toward the ocean. I realized he was speaking Spanish and told him, "*No habla espanol.*" The man then looked at the ocean and then at my wife, saying, "I'm sorry I thought those two Mexican boys were yours because you looked Mexican, but now I don't see those two boys." I told the man I never even saw the two boys the entire time I was facing the ocean.

My wife and I both started tearing up as the man kept saying, "I could have sworn there were two boys out there yelling at you for help," and while listening to him, I heard that voice, "It's me, your Lord." As best we could between the tears, we started to share what we were currently going through as we realized we would be going to be asked to officially file for adoption and the struggle that would cause in our family. Just like you would expect from a higher power, divine intervention set in as suddenly this man's words became needed wisdom. The man made it clear: "First, you are doing the right thing. Those boys are your first priority. They need your help to protect them and raise them." The man shared that family, especially by blood, will always want to try to fix everything. However, they can't, especially when drugs are involved. The man declared that we must realize that we may lose the strong relationship with the family since they won't agree with the idea of keeping the boys away from the birth parents in order to protect them from drugs. It was the right thing to do for the boys, and we must stick by the boys even if it means losing our family.

As we sat there on Eagle Beach with the man, his family joined, and I could just feel the love this man had for his family and how sincere he was being with us. We shared how blessed we were and how Aruba had led us to our Catholic faith. Now Aruba was giving us the needed signs to move on with our journey with these two boys. We realized that our two girls were the ones who said from the beginning, "You must take care of them," and how they were the reason for our Catholic faith today. We shared how amazing it was that our friends' timeshare resort was here on Eagle Beach, which led to this very moment, where we were blessed to have met him because he saw two boys who needed help from us in the ocean.

Ironically, none of us, including his family, ever saw the two boys in the ocean that he was yelling to us about. I knew the higher power had put these two boys in that man's vision, which represented the two boys we were going to adopt. As the conversation was coming to a close, and sunset turned into night, we hugged each other, and I asked the man, "What's your name?" He humbly replied, "Rocco Paternasto. I am from New Jersey." After sharing with him our names, I stood in awe as he walked off with his family. I was shaking because I knew his name was of Latin descent.

Thanks to mobile phones, I called my daughter who had been studying Latin as part of her Catholic high school education. Immediately, my daughter says, "*Rocco Paternasto* means Father of the Rock," which was Jesus's disciple, Peter, or basically like God's foundation. At that moment, the joy and blessing overwhelmed me as I stood there on Eagle Beach. The higher power who, along with Grandma Lestie, was teaching me the need to help others gave me the greatest gift of all, which was the sign that two boys needed our help. That same higher power put it in Rocco Paternasto's mind and heart to yell help for those boys, and then remind us why it was so important. That meant it was okay losing the support of our extended family in the process.

Every time we had struggles in our family because of those two boys, I always came back to that sunset in Aruba with such a clear sign from the higher power—the sign being those boys needed our help. I realize more and more that my dad's lesson, "All of us believe in a higher power," was way more than just religion, especially organized religion.

> **Life lesson: Dad's lesson was more about we all have a need for faith, and this comes from our common desire to seek a higher power. The interesting part is when you realize that he's everywhere, and he provides signs as we allow ourselves to be open to listen and help each other.**

That lesson came to light as we were heading toward the closing of our new home on 12324 Gaines Way. I had listened to my heart to go ahead and call on a house that was clearly a pending sale, then moved forward because of front porch advice from my dad: "If you keep doing what you have been doing, then you'll keep getting what you have been getting." Then ironically, to cold-call for financing on that house based on another heartfelt message of "Go ahead and call," which led to a callback from a lady at the finance office whose husband I knew. That lady helped us get 100 percent financing approval on a house that needed a lot of love, even though we owned three properties with mortgages at the time. In return for all that help, we suddenly knew why two boys needed emergency foster care. This was the call for help we received shortly after receiving confirmation of a confirmed closing on our new home and for the sale of our existing three properties.

I remember sitting there after the phone calls, thinking, *Lord, you have really blessed us*. Months later, as I walking up to our mailbox on Gaines Way, I saw the *12324* and heard him saying, "The 1 became 2, then another came to make 3, and now 2 more have come to finally make 4." At that moment, the higher power gave me a sign to let me know he had taken care of us. We had done what he needed us to do by choosing to help two boys, and in return, he had helped us by getting us to a place where we could raise them. My dad's life lessons were ringing true.

I grew up watching my parents go to their Hillsboro hometown every weekend they could. As I reflect back on those trips, I now realize it was more about helping their family than about getting time to catch up and just visit family. I remember my mom making sure that Grandma Lestie had enough groceries, and I now know how modest my parents' income was at the time. I now recognize that the higher power was right there for as she tried to help, and suddenly, out of nowhere, my cousins would show up with surplus treasures they had to give Grandma Lestie as well.

Similarly, my dad would be fixing broken doors, cabinets, sinks, tubs, toilets, furnaces, drains, gutters, and anything else he found at Grandma Lestie's house that needed repair while we were there. I would be with him the following week at the local salvage yard, looking through throwaways from home demolitions to find pieces and parts to put things back together, again for the least amount of cost. This included trips to the Bargain Barn, which is similar to today's Big Lots, to find new pieces when none could be salvaged from old ones.

Once we finished up at Grandma Lestie's, then we would head over to my grandpa OG's house. In similar fashion, I would watch my dad take care of repairing things he could around the house. My mom would be going through all his medicines to make sure he had them straight, marking the bottles in a way so he could remember.

As part of those many trips, mostly on my dad's taking a day off, which was Sunday. In the background, there would be hymns from either the car radio, my grandpa OG's house radio, or perhaps a cousin who came by to visit at Grandma Lestie's with their guitar. I felt such peace and happiness in those moments as I sat there and listened. At the time, I had those moments of "Why do we need to spend so much time here?" But I now realize that the higher power was showing himself through my parents helping their family.

Growing up with the many trips to Hillsboro, Ohio, I heard about Uncle Willard, especially since he was a celebrity in the town from being on the local radio station. At the time, he was very busy with the radio station as well as owning the Hillsboro Sundry Store with his wife and, of course, raising his own family. In recent years, he and I became very close, for we both were driven and enjoyed talking about business. Both of us were what they call today "entrepreneurs." My life lessons from him always seemed to end with statements like, "And don't forget the man upstairs." At the time, I had not recognized that once again, Dad was right, for Uncle Willard's higher power was simply known as "the man upstairs."

It all made sense to me as we were enjoying his retirement from radio after sixty-two years. At his celebration held at a local church in Hillsboro, I began to learn about the many things Uncle Willard had done for the community. During a major snowstorm in 1978, Uncle Willard was camped out at the radio station even though many had not gone to work due to over three feet of snowfall in about a thirty-three-hour period. As the calls came in from listeners learning about people being trapped in their homes, Uncle Willard contacted the local fire department. The department could not respond to the people in need because they had no snowmobiles to get through the snow. Using the power of the radio, Uncle Willard declared a need to raise money to help the fire department and EMTs purchase the much-needed snowmobiles to help the trapped citizens of the community. Within hours, donations from citizens and local businesses helped raise the money, and the fire department was soon equipped with snowmobiles.

As I listened further at Uncle Willard's retirement celebration, I heard several major radio announcers share their appreciation for Willard's bringing them up in radio. Because of him, their lives were forever changed. Similarly, I listened to retired school principals, mayors, and grownups of the community all sharing their great memories of getting up in the morning to hear Willard Park say, "WSRW. Hillsboro, Ohio—the voice of southern Ohio."

At the end of Uncle Willard's celebration, my life lesson came when he shared all the great people who had helped him. One of them was the first station owner, David Winslow. Winslow had heard his voice while sitting in the Highland County Courthouse. As he shared his many blessings in life due to radio, many in the audience would call out and remind him of what he had done for them. After making his final signoff of "WSRW. Hillsboro, Ohio," as requested by the audience, he pointed and looked up, saying "To God be the glory." At that very moment, I knew that Uncle Willard's "man upstairs" was him believing in God himself. As Dad says, "We all believe in a higher power." As the emotions of that moment rushed in, I truly realized my uncle's love and respect for the higher power.

Life lesson: Always respect and recognize the higher power's blessings by showing respect for him even in front of folks who may even consider you a celebrity.

Uncle Willard made no hesitation to recognize God in front of everyone. From that moment on, I wondered, *Do the people around me know I too believe in a higher power? Have I ever shared with my coworkers my blessings from God? Do my kids realize how I believe in a higher power?* As I have begun to share my belief in a higher power, I have been so excited to learn how many others admit to the same—with some even surprising me at their commitment to the higher power, like helping on Sundays with readings and being greeters and ushers.

I would have never imagined the truth in Dad's "We all believe in a higher power" until I actually started sharing myself. Thanks to that moment with my uncle that taught me it's good to share our thanks to God, for it not only leads you in helping others but also leads in others helping you. It is interesting to realize that in sharing my moments and signs of a higher power that people helping people is where God is trying to teach us that we all should believe in a higher power. I now wonder if that is where my dad learned his life lesson of "We all believe in a higher power," as he was helping others, and they were helping him. This belief in a higher power has led me to being interested to at least understand the other higher power found in the various religions today.

As I continued to hunger to learn about the higher power, I was fascinated with the history of the church. I'm beginning to understand how most organized religions agree on the lineage up to Abraham. It is interesting from there that Christians follow on to the Messiah, Jesus Christ, while the Jews don't believe that the Messiah has come yet. On the other hand, the Muslim's leader Muhammad was from the lineage of Abraham also. It was these new understandings that led me to reading the Torah, which is focused on the first five books of the Bible where the law of the church prevails. In addition, I picked up a copy of the Book of Mormon in Salt Lake City, Utah, and was fascinated that similar to the Course of Miracles that God was saying to their leader, "I want the people of today to know that I am a living God."

As I ponder all organized religion, I see the common thread of God or, as Dad would say, a higher power. As I listen to various Christian music I hear "God's not dead," and as I read the various Bibles, I must admit that seems to be the message from the "I Am." It seems we could all learn from each other if we just focused on the higher power. As I am learning every day from my grandsons, this world is an amazing and beautiful place.

As I watch my grandsons stand in awe of animals like the giraffe, asking, "Why do they have such long necks?" or stand in awe of the gorillas and lions, asking, "Why do they roar?" I have begun to have that same awe and wonder as they do.

As I was walking the Biltmore estate grounds, I stood in awe as I began to really look and consider all the different sizes, barks, shapes of leaves, and even the shapes of the trees themselves. As I walked the trails on the shores of Lake Tahoe, I stood in awe at the inspiring height of the cedars and pines of the region. As I walked the Yosemite Valley to see Veil Falls, I stood in awe at the size of the granite-covered mountains and the pure beauty of the trees, and the smell of the air. As I watched the sunset over the tranquil Marco Island, I stood in awe as I basked in the warm glow of the sun. As I sat beside the running creeks of the Smoky Mountains, I sat in awe of the peace found just being bathed in the sound of the waterfalls.

As I played in the sands of beaches with my grandsons, I too have been in awe of how beautiful and fun it is to be in the sand. As I enjoyed the heavens from the window of a nighttime plane, I sat in awe of the twinkling stars that are there every time. As I walked the streets of Rome, Italy, I stood in awe of St. Peter's Cathedral and knowing that God's disciple Peter is even buried there below. As I walked the streets of Florence, Italy, I stood in awe of the statue *David* by Michelangelo. As I walked the streets of Assisi, Italy, I stood in awe as I realized St. Francis walked and lived in the places where I was visiting.

As I consider all these amazing places and things, I began to wonder, "How can there not be a God?" It is hard to imagine that man on his own right dreamed up these things or that they just happened through evolutions and great storms. Who then created the great storms or the things that caused them?

> **Life lesson: As I breathe in more life experiences, I recognize that there must be a God or a higher power, for this comes not just from what I see and study intentionally, but it comes also from things which are not intentional, such as signs or unplanned events or coincidences.**

How do you explain signs from nowhere? Like the man needing thirty-five cents at Crater Lake; like the man needing twenty dollars along the road to the Detroit Airport; like the man who thought our two boys needed help in the waters of Aruba's Eagle Beach; or like me having the need to buy a house that was already pending.

I can only justify these signs or events as being somehow organized so that I could be given the chance to recognize them, even as a simple human being. That organization came from somewhere, and that leads me to what my dad calls best as the higher power. As I now organize my thoughts and write them down, I recognize more that my dad was right in saying that we all believe in a higher power.

How else do we find a way to see and enjoy the beauty that is all around us? How amazing is it that kids come along to remind us of the awe and beauty of things that have been covered up by being a serious adult?

I do not think it was an accident that humans have a natural cycle that allows us to have so much time at the beginning as a child and returning again as a senior adult. We manage to get sidetracked in the middle with the seriousness of the so-called life. I now have begun to rediscover the beauty and awe of the world as I see it and hear it through the lives of my grandsons. Now that I understand the beauty of the world again, I can truly say Dad was right, and that higher power is found everywhere in what we see and especially in what we see as we help others.

WORK IS A PART OF LIFE, SO GET USED TO IT

The first time I heard dad saying, "Work is a part of life, so get used to it," I was on the way to one of my many painting jobs. I was around twelve years old, and I was waving goodbye to my friends who were playing outside. I asked Dad, "Why don't they have to go to work?" It's funny because I don't remember arguing with him about it, and I kind of remember thinking, *Well, okay, I guess*. My dad was not only my dad but also my best friend and coworker, for we spent every evening together while my mom worked at GC Murphy's.

Growing up with him, I recall my mom dropping me off at the paper mill when he worked overtime and riding on the tow motor with him as he got orders ready to ship the next day. At six years old, who gets to ride around and learn about forklifts and making paper envelopes? Not many kids likely today due to the OSHA rules. It's interesting too that being with a dad who used his hands led me to being the neighborhood "Mr. Fix-It" for bicycles. All the kids knew I could fix things, and my dad loved it when I used his tools.

For my sixth birthday, I received a twenty-one-inch Toro power-driven lawn mower, to which my dad lowered the handles so I could reach them. My friend's mom across the street named Rita even mentioned to my mom how dangerous it is for a six-year-old to mow the grass, and her reply was, "He knows the dangers. His dad taught him, and it's none of your business," and that was the end of the conversation. It was in the 1970s when people would not just call social services and register a complaint like they most likely would likely today.

As I reflect on those friends across the street—the ones who did not mow the grass or paint with their dad as a job—they ended up in trouble with the law and drugs. Furthermore, more of those friends just down the street were twins who really got messed up on drugs. One twin brother committed suicide in my high school senior year. The twin sister was found overdosed in some bushes not far away from their home as well. I realize now that my dad's "Work is a part of life, so get used to it" was all about establishing good habits, like working versus having bad habits like drug abuse. Even in junior high, I remember a friend who stole cars before school to make money, then used that money to buy, use, and sell drugs. He explained to me how *easy* the money was, but I truly already had it in my mind that work is a part of life, and that I should get used to it, so I just never considered easy to be a good formula for work.

It's funny too how growing up with a dad who always had more than one job never complained about going to work. I will always remember those dark, early mornings of coffee and toast folded in half by the butter knife to make it a quick bite to eat, and that happy "Are you ready?" as we would head off down the steps on a Saturday morning to get in a full day of painting or remodeling a porch or room for somebody.

As I got into high school, my lifelong best friend joined us in painting houses as well. We realize now how my dad would put us on the hottest side of the house on

Saturday mornings. He knew we had been out partying the night before, so he would help us sweat out our adventures from the night before. As usual, my dad never revealed his strategy, but he would come over to check on us with a cold glass of water and say, "You boys all right? You might want to get some water." That comment made me realize that dad knew we were hungover and sweating it out, so that's why were on the sunny side of the house.

At the time, my lifelong friend and I were working at a grocery store and painting houses with my dad, which we did all through college, even when we were both co-opping at General Motors. In retrospect, my dad's work habits was burned in me, for I never gave a second thought that I was working more than one job, just like my dad had shown me growing up.

As my career started in manufacturing after college, I found myself volunteering to be a maintenance crew leader on the weekends, even though I was a full-time engineer all week. At the time, I didn't see it as a second job, but in hindsight, it truly was once again. To me, it seemed natural to accept extra work. I really enjoyed the "how to make it and keep it running" side of the manufacturing business. Like my dad cleaning and organizing paintbrushes for the next day, I found myself studying for the upcoming weekend work, making sure we had the parts, tools, and equipment needed to be ready to get at it on Saturday.

As I began to learn about manufacturing equipment, I found myself laying out the details of the work to make sure we did not miss anything. This habit of checking details was like watching my dad counting skids and organizing them in the paper mill for the next day's shipments. As the work got started on the weekends, it felt natural to check on the team, just like what my dad did for me. Like Dad, I would find myself asking the maintenance team members, "You boys alright?" On those Saturday mornings, my dad would sometimes hear from us, "Do you know where the trim paint is?" on his check-ins, and then he would go get it happily as he would say, "Now you can keep going." In a similar fashion to my dad, I would happily take off to get a missing drawing, double-check a dimension, or replace a needed part that was just found broken from the general stores, which was located inside the plant to keep the weekend work moving along.

> **Life lesson: My dad's work motto was about establishing good habits and great fundamentals of working as a team.**

I'm now realizing as I am putting together these writings and reflecting on those life lessons the value of his simple but powerful words. I never had a doubt that my dad would show up to work on a paint or remodeling job. I always knew he would figure a way out of an issue, whether it was, "How are we going to paint that?" or "How are going to fix that?" As usual, after such questions, he would disappear into our toolbox or a local hardware store and come back with a solution that always worked out. Even if those fixes took a "a little umph," as Dad would say, he went to work on implementing the solution. I realize now that work was my dad's educational institution where he was the professor, and I was the student.

I now recognize that my dad taught me that work was way more than just making money. It was about doing what's right. I believe that's why the sentence ended with "so get used to it." It is about getting used to not only having a good habit but also about adding value. My dad never worried about how much he made on a job. His major focus was on doing what was right and making sure the customer was satisfied. This is why the Toyota Way of "Customer first" makes so much sense and seems natural to me. It's not a burden to make the time to get a project right, whether I get paid for it or not. For as Dad taught me, "It's about adding value." It's about spending time with the customer and making sure they are satisfied by making sure you met their expectations.

Dad's opening part of his statement "Work is life" adds to the importance of adding value. As we learned from mathematical word problems, the word *is* translates to the equal sign (=). So "Work is life" translates to "Work *equals* life," which better shows the importance of the need for work. Without work or adding value, we cannot expect life or more exactly a good life. Why? When we do not work, then we're not making a difference in the world for ourselves and especially for others. We tend to feel a sense of accomplishment or the feeling of a good life when we see things get accomplished or come together like those houses we painted. What was once a peeling and faded structure now had a new life as the mixture of new colors brought back its beauty. At the same time, we watched those homeowners smile with pride as they saw their newly painted home and thanking us and not just paying us for all the hard work that made their home beautiful. I have those same feelings today as I watch our new building expansions come up out of the ground at Toyota.

Those feelings make so much sense. Working is like breathing or eating for a human. Work is just a fundamental need to sustain our life and ultimately the life of others. If you realize that work is energy from the laws of physics, then "work equals life" takes on a much deeper meaning as you look at the world that the higher power created for us. It takes energy or work for the trees to grow. They need water and nutrients from the ground to survive, and conversely, the trees give us life by converting carbon dioxide into oxygen. It takes energy or work for the sun to help the trees process the nutrients, and conversely, the shade created by those leaves absorbing the sun's light allows humans to naturally have a place to cool off.

It takes energy or work for the various crops to grow, and conversely, those crops feed us and the animals that also feed us in various ways. It takes energy or work to create the power that feeds our homes, and conversely, that same power enriches our life whether it's lights to see at night, chill for those hot summer days, or heat for cold winter days. It takes energy or work to create the power that feeds our transportation, and conversely, that same power allows our automobiles, airplanes, and various wheeled devices to take us places, whether it's for our own work, vacation, shopping, or visiting with family and friends.

I truly appreciate the power of my dad's words now more than ever and how important each word was that he used in those frequent sayings of his while I was growing up. Just as we can understand life by applying some forms of math and physics, I realize now that there is a necessity in work, for again, it's not about making money but also about adding value. For even our higher power provides us with so many examples of how work or energy is adding value to our planet and ultimately to each of us in the process as well. How could I have known that my dad's life lesson could have had so much meaning as I now realize it does. I now understand even more why I get so frustrated when I hear others complain about work, because I truly know the value of work and accept it as a fundamental principle.

For me, work is truly something that I consider as natural as breathing, and it's as essential as breathing is for giving life to the cells inside our body. That same work gives me that feeling of accomplishment, which leads to a happy life and sense of pride, especially when I take the time to make sure the job is done right. Work, for me, has been something that I've gotten used to because I'm driven by the habit of receiving and giving value to myself and others as I complete the work. Even while I'm working, I can't help but multitask—thinking and organizing the next thing that I want to work on. They say you never work if you're doing something you love or enjoy. I believe this idea comes from the fact that what we love is to add value or to make a difference in this world, especially when it's something beyond ourselves. The object of our work does have a value that is not intrinsic, especially when the object helps others accomplish something, whether it's a place to live, a place to enjoy, or a thing that allows people to be productive or enjoy the world through the use of it. My dad's lesson on work truly is an important one for having a good life, or as he would say, "Work is life."

Another dimension to Dad's work ethic is about how the higher power puts thoughts in our minds to accomplish things. For myself, the house at 12324 was a constant work in progress, but I just had this inner desire to leave it better than I found it. I remember the first year of putting the kitchen together, finding kitchen cabinets in a flea-market-type paper for $5,000 that were my wife's favorite white color. Upon going to look at them in Anderson Township, Ohio, I found that they were beautiful Wood-Mode cabinets made in Kreamer, Pennsylvania, and were forty-two inches high, which was perfect for our high ceilings. I had them picked up and delivered to our basement so I could figure out the layout, since the kitchen corners had forty-five-degree angles. I managed to make a layout to use all but one cabinet, and it was beautiful. Why do I share such detail? It seems strange that a 12324 house that was "pending" for four and a half years now has beautiful kitchen cabinets in it, and all because of a long-held desire inside me for a house on a hill with white pillars, which it does now have. However, if the higher power's desire is for us to add value, then why not have that value also be for good? As I look back at that beautiful white kitchen now, I see the good in the many meals it held, whether it was for a birthday, graduation, shower, Thanksgiving, or Christmas. Good not only for me, but especially for my family, their many friends, and our extended family.

Similar to 12324, my dad bought his family home out of a foreclosure, after the builder had gone bankrupt. Like me, my dad had to finish putting the house in Miamisburg, Ohio, together, for it was only studs with an incomplete layout. In my first six months of life, my dad and brother were finishing enough of that house so we could all move in. In similar fashion, I have so many memories of events, like birthdays, my parents' twenty-fifth wedding anniversary, Thanksgivings, and Christmases. Our house in Miamisburg, Ohio, was the regular stop for my uncle Ralph and my favorite cousins, Steve and Wayman. I remember the hearty laugh of Uncle Ralph as we watched the Jerry Lewis movie *The Geisha Boy* and cracking up at the white rabbit sunbathing, which seemed to be on during every Thanksgiving visit. I remember the many pies we had to choose over that were made by Mom and Aunt Martha, and were quickly devoured by the rest of our extended family who would show up on Thanksgiving Day, especially Uncle Russell and his wife, Aunt Hazel.

Once again, I realize that my dad added not only value to that house in Miamisburg but also created amazing good for the many people who visited there, and that this good is truly what the higher power is looking for from the things that we add value to.

Looking around and studying others, I have begun to recognize the connection of adding value and good for people. One of my favorite mentors is Walt Disney. Walt acted on an inner desire to create an amusement park for families after he had taken his daughters to a local carnival and saw how terribly dirty and poorly run the carnivals were. From that moment, Walt was on a mission that led to Disneyland in California. Not satisfied with the result, because the area adjacent to Disneyland became crammed with hotels and stores that were poorly run, making it difficult to maintain the image of a beautiful and magical place for family, Walt knew he needed a new and larger space to create his dream.

Walt quietly pursued his dream of Disney World in Florida, thanks to the great commitment and financing of his brother Roy. I can only imagine that Walt had no idea how many families with kids he would impact on a daily basis. Walt's desire was to add value by creating an amusement park for families to have fun in a safe place and use their imagination at a place large enough that it would never stop growing and changing, like the landscape. Disney World today averages around fifty-seven thousand visitors per day, and that does not even consider the daily attendance at Disneyland, Disney Europe, Disney China, and the other Disney sites and their cruises. As a fan of Disney myself, I have experienced the good from the value created by Walt Disney, as I have watched my own kids' dreams come to life as they experience the World of Disney. I see that same good in the eyes of the families alongside us inside at the World of Disney.

I have studied Henry Ford, and I realize the impact of his desire to build a car that every man could afford. Ford's desire led to his company having 90 percent of the world's automobiles by 1914 after just starting up in 1903. Ford's adding value by making automobiles affordable led to the creation of roads, highways, gas stations, and all the infrastructure that supports the automobile transportation industry. Considering that people use automobiles to go to work and to move goods for work and friends and so on, I can't even fathom the amount of good created by the automobile that truly comes from the desire of Henry

Ford wanting to add value by making an automobile that every man could afford. Along the way, he also developed the assembly line, which revolutionized the manufacturing world for all goods.

I believe each of us can add value and create good just by being willing to move forward with our inner desires that require effort, if we keep in mind my dad's work ideals. A simpler example is George Vanderbilt and his desire to build the Biltmore Estate in Asheville, North Carolina. George's desire was to build an estate for his family and his closest friends to enjoy the finer things in life, so his true thought of adding value was for a small group of people. As I have read the letters of those who visited the estate early on, I could hear the good George created as they shared the joys of the wonderful food, relaxing afternoon walks in the woods, and the fun of playing games on the lawn and inside the Biltmore house.

Today, the Biltmore Estate, run by his grandchildren, is a bustling destination with annual attendance of over a million visitors. Due to George's desire to add value to his family and his closest friends, his dream has now expanded to over a million people annually. I'm sure George could not imagine the good created every day as people get to see and feel the lives of a wealthy family. Visitors get to enjoy some of the amazing food the Vanderbilts and their friends enjoyed years ago, like they were guests of the family.

As a fan of the Biltmore Estate and an annual pass holder, I have enjoyed the good as a Biltmore guest with my family and friends. Similarly, I see the other Biltmore visitors' eyes light up as they experience the first views of the house from the drive entrance or the massiveness of the Grand Dinner Hall, or the beautiful details in the architecture found in each room, or the amazing art and furniture George collected in his travels around the world.

As I have progressed in my career at Toyota, the key to doing so was by adding value. While making progress in assembly, I spent the time to create the AMS, or the Assembly Machine Standards, so I could make sure that the lessons we learned were captured and documented to eliminate repeat issues in the future. Our project board standard for project management in assembly is now in the TCSR, or Toyota Construction Safety Requirements, for all engineers at Toyota to follow when doing projects at the plants.

While moving the powertrain from ninety-day to nine-day shutdowns, I introduced the *Denwacho*, or hourly schedule from assembly, to ensure clear plans for the weekend were made so the Monday morning start-ups went well. I established a technician group as well to work on the modifications of existing equipment, which required following not only the detailed instructions from the machine maker but also the required modifications to existing parts to make everything work together successfully.

To ensure success in my career, results were important, but adding value along the way was important as well. It seems that Dad's words really connects the desire to add value and ultimately do good for people, which leads to a good life. My time in the facilities group included adding value by making sure our project teams had the right amount of support from subject matter experts who made sure we were properly constructing buildings.

Similarly, in my dealing with real estate, I realize now that the key to success was not just about getting results, which is about having tenants, but also about making a difference in the community. By improving each unit as it was vacated and thus adding value, we were able to provide a better product to new tenants, and ultimately, that allowed us to ask for better rents, which allowed us to do more for the property. As we reinvested, and better tenants moved in, we were able to further improve the exterior of the property and the amenities. At the time, we had no idea of the impact until a local community member saw us in Lowe's and stopped us, saying, "We are so happy for all the work you've done on Mohawk Trail. It's completely changed the whole look of the street." At that moment, we realized our work on those apartment buildings was going beyond our own space and truly was for the good of the community. We found similar results on another property we had in Cheviot. As we began to repair things, the existing tenants also shared the issues they had in their units and improved their upkeep on the property. As this evolved, our tenants began to thank us, saying, "You're the best landlords we have ever had because you care about taking care of things."

In addition, the local police of Cheviot expressed their appreciation for us for making sure our tenants respected each other, which ultimately led to reduced issues from our property. Once again, adding value in the form of making repairs moved beyond just our property and was doing good for the community. Considering these examples from my dad and myself, whether for our families or careers, the value we added soon multiplied—it created good for others, which then multiplied as the good and then expanded beyond them too. My hope is that as people feel good about adding value, they too will want to put in work of their own and, in return, add more value. I believe this is the key to getting a community to be productive. If a group of people recognize the good from adding value, then they will soon want to do more themselves and ultimately for others as well.

> **Life lesson:** As I reflect on successful projects, I see a similar pattern of the team adding value for other team members, who, in turn, create good for other people, which then perpetuates further

when they are motivated to add value and do good as well.

It seems natural that the higher power, who also created value in creating the world around us, would also expect us to work. It seems his efforts to create beautiful places and things are well beyond the basics of just doing work. His idea of value must be one of creating good. I realize this more and more as I look more closely at nature. For example, if trees were only for shade, then what is the value of having so many kinds of trees? I believe the higher power recognized the good in having trees in different sizes and shapes—not just for function, but also for the good that would be manifested in people as they enjoyed their beauty.

As I look at the various animals like fish, I think that if fish were only there to fill the waters with food, then what is the value of having so many different kinds of fish? I believe the higher power knew the value of his people wanting to discover the beauty hidden in the depths of the water, and that discovery would be the good that comes from those people enjoying the beauty of the many species of fish on their journey.

Even as I travel and meet people, I realize the amount of work that the "higher power" put into each and every one of us. Not only do we all have unique features, like hair color, eye color, height differences, skin color, and shape differences, but we have also unique styles of communication through language and writing; unique ways of learning through our senses of sight, smell, and touch; unique ways of working together through individuals and teams; unique ways of dressing, whether simple or sophisticated; and unique beliefs or values that seem way beyond the need of just being a human. If that was our purpose from the higher power, the higher power clearly has a high sense of adding value.

I now have begun to realize the good that comes from differences. I believe the higher power knows the beauty that is found in discovering and understanding differences. I believe that is why he went to great lengths and incorporated all the subtle things you can find in nature, as I continue to study the world and zoom in on individual things. The details I find are truly amazing. I ponder over why God took such time to detail the wings of a butterfly or the details of the back of a shagbark hickory tree. I feel the same when I look out over the valley created by Lake Tahoe and wonder how God decided to put this here. and why God decided to make such enormous pines at this location versus somewhere else. I feel the same when I look out over the heavens of an airplane window and realize how amazing it is that the higher power put the desire of flight into humans, and more importantly, the physics like a Bernoulli equation into a human's mind to figure out how to create lift on a man-made wing.

I feel the same when I enjoy the beauty of a light bulb in the early morning hours as I get to work on a new creation and ponder how amazing it is that the higher power not only helped humans imagine how to make a light bulb but also gave them the ability to make the power from natural resources like water and natural gas to create the electricity needed for them to be lit.

I feel the same as I enjoy water from a spigot that is clean and even hot when I need it. It's amazing to think how the higher power inspired humans to want to make water towers to not only store clean water but also to use that storage to pressurize the system, minimizing the size of pumps in the system as well, and then to further inspire a human to develop water heaters so that we could have hot water on demand versus having to make a fire and have to wait on it to get hot first.

I realize now that the core of adding value is making a difference. The difference starts with the idea of changing things. In that journey, we add value when those changes create good for someone or something that ultimately helps someone.

Life lesson: I am beginning to understand that the real value of work comes in the good that comes from it—not only for ourselves, but most importantly for others.

From this good, the higher power expects that more will come from it as the receiver will then feel the good and be motivated as well to add value in some way.

I wonder if my dad knew how his profound words were really the fundamentals that the higher power wanted his people to know and understand. "Work equals life" shows that life manifests itself through work, for its value then provides good to ourselves and others.

The "getting used to it" will ultimately create the situation where all of us want to do good for ourselves and others. As these words are living out for us and others, we will then realize the ultimate world. Then I wonder if that is the heaven that the higher power writes about. If we continually saw work as doing good, I wonder how different our world could be from today. I wonder if there would be no more hunger, as people would be helping ourselves and others to create food. I wonder if there would be no more homeless, as people would be helping themselves and others to create shelter. I wonder if there would be no more water shortages, as people would be willing to help ourselves and others create wells and reservoirs to make sure there is enough water.

I wonder if there would be no more fighting among people since we would all be satisfied by having all that we needed by helping ourselves and each other. It seems like having the idea of "Work is life, so get used to it" as a fundamental belief would lead to nirvana where, suddenly, everyone would naturally get along, and all the people would be satisfied. I believe my dad had that in mind, for he himself lived the same way. He always seemed satisfied, and he got along with everyone. It seems his words helped him to live a successful and happy life.

For myself, I admit that I'm the happiest when I'm productive and helping myself and others to build things or fix things. I believe that like our Creator, the higher power, we have this internal desire to create things. As I consider this further, I believe that is why "work is life" or "work equals life" is so right for people and "getting used to it" represents the value or good coming from the work, and it becomes something that we desire for ourselves and others. As we feel good about what we've created, then it will naturally motivate us to do more good or add value so we will get used to it and therefore carry us forward to more. Thanks, Dad, for your life lesson and amazing worlds to live by each and every day.

WORK NEVER KILLED NOBODY

I'm now realizing how my dad's words, "Work never killed nobody," were as necessary as his other words, "Work is life, so get used to it." Why? For someone who has never experienced value from work, how do you get started working or be motivated enough to do it? Growing up hearing those words, I would often be assuming that the person was already working and would be constantly looking at the effort of themselves or others worrying that work was actually impacting that person's well-being or health. For myself, the words were *self-motivation* or *perseverance* to keep going at whatever I was working on, like shredding up the willow trees from around the pond in the dead heat of summer. I would stop just long enough for a glass of water while my brothers-in-law, who were almost ten years younger than me, got severe headaches and nausea after a few hours of working with me.

In my mind, whether I worked out for hours in the heat of summer on something for our family, or stayed up all night in the factory to complete a project, I would say to myself proudly, "I'm the Clydesdale of the human race." My dad's words were the reason I worked thirty-two hours straight to not only finish my project at the

Georgetown, Kentucky, plant, but also to stay all night to finish a project for my coworker who was struggling due to many pieces of equipment being torn down at the same time. Those same words drove me to work nine-day shutdowns, where it was an honor to do all the work I could to ensure things were completed and ready for the start-up at the beginning of the New Year.

It was those words that led me to believe in work and honor it with words like Aaron Tippin's song, "I have a working man's PhD." I knew in my mind that both sides of my family were farmers, for both sides of grandparents grew tobacco. I saw pictures of them in tobacco fields and knew the hardship that they and the Appalachian people had gone through to even have a farm or place to raise a family. I knew from my mom that my great Grandpa Parr only had one arm, but with that, he not only built himself a house but also a barn. I knew that my dad, who farmed till he was thirty-two years old, was known to drive his old Farmall tractor all night long. My mom shared how she would look out into the fields for his headlights confirming that he was still moving along. My mom drove a tractor at the age of twelve all day long to earn a dollar so she could save up and buy her dad insulin to help him treat his emphysema.

It was those words that would make me proud to be sore and have blisters from a hard day's work. I was following in my dad's and my family's footsteps. I could see the years of work in the hands of my dad, mom, grandma Lestie, and grandpa Ogle Glenn. At the same time that I saw the impact of hard work, I would always hear pride from them for having to do the work. Grandma Lestie didn't only talk about canning food. I would be there with her snapping beans or shucking corn, realizing the work required but not even considering it as work. Listening to the stories she shared and the pride she had in how many jars were made or how many jars she had given away made it a treat to help. Similarly, at home, I would help Dad and Mom can green beans or pick apples, strawberries, and grapes. I loved the smell of my mom making grape jelly from the vines in our own backyard after spending the morning picking them and smashing them in preparation for jelly.

I saw the words of my dad lived out as we would break down those skids he brought home from the paper mill. We removed the nails, cut them to length to span the trusses, and made sure there was enough of them to cover the roof of the kitchen that my dad was adding on at Grandma Lestie's house. We cut down trees with my brother and his father-in-law behind what was to be the parking lots of the Dayton Mall. Cutting those trees up and splitting them and then carrying them sixty yards to the nearby pickup truck bed was like living through my Appalachian heritage, where I learned the great stories of Daniel Boone and Simon Kenton as we worked.

I saw those words every fall as my dad brought home skids from the paper mill to break down, cut to length, and use them in our fireplace in the basement for those wonderful, crackling fires on the cold winter mornings.

I saw those words when my dad would break down the wood skids from the paper mill, then turn them into TV stands, cabinets, shelves, and knickknack holders for my mom, family, and friends. Watching those big, worn hands taking care to remove the nails, filling in the holes with wood putty, and sanding them smooth by hand was like watching a master craftsman.

I saw those words at work when I would watch and help my dad work on cars, whether it was changing oil, hand-grinding engine valves, hand-honing a cylinder bore, or going through a pile of used tires to find the best ones for our vehicle so we would be on the road again to another day's work or vacation.

I saw those words as my dad would find time to begin building his woodshop in our backyard. Seeing the floor, then the walls, and finally the roof come together was just amazing, and I imagined Noah building the Ark and the accomplishment he must have felt once it was done.

I saw those words as my dad built a bathroom in our basement. I was fascinated how those pile of two-by-fours became floors, walls, and ultimately led to space that was now useful. I now wonder about the effort this space required while he worked overtime at the paper mill and painted and remodeled houses. It seems the idea of "Work never killed nobody" was true for my dad and my family, for they were living proof of it.

I saw those words as my dad built a carport beside our house. His resolve to finish it became even clearer when it collapsed about halfway through installing the trusses. My dad and I even got hurt, which led to some stitches for me, but that afternoon, he was back at it. I sat in a lawn chair as my dad took the carport pieces apart and rebuilt them. His determination was clear, and his only emotion was worry for me getting hurt, but I don't recall a word of frustration for any of it coming down.

As I reflect on myself, I see those words coming out as well. My soon-to-be wife had bought an almost twenty-year-old mobile home from an elderly couple, so it needed work. I remember donning coveralls and crawling around underneath to reinstall new insulation so it would be more energy-efficient, and I don't recall complaining about cobwebs or the filthy messes I had to clean out to get to it. I remember us painting the outside of it and the shed, with my wife spilling a gallon of the paint, and we just kept right on going to the finish. I remember reworking the steps to the front door so we could park one of our vehicles under the carport, especially since parking space was so limited. That perseverance paid off. Four years later, we received enough money from it to buy our first home.

I saw those words as we moved into our first house on Lea Avenue in Miamisburg, Ohio. I finished the laundry room so my wife could enjoy doing laundry and not feel like she was working at a partial rehab. I rebuilt the deck, making it larger for gatherings, and added lighting so we could enjoy evenings there as well. Once again, those efforts paid off four years later as we sold it in a few days for the full asking price of $99,900 after originally buying it for $83,000.

I saw those words when we bought our first house in Michigan on Cheryl Drive. The house was dated and covered from end to end with wallpaper. While my wife focused on removing wallpaper, I reorganized the wall of the kitchen to obtain better use of the living room and the open floor plan. We were only there for thirteen months, which included the delivery of our second child, but once again, the efforts paid off, for it sold within days for $139,900 after just buying it for $119,000.

I saw those words as we purchased our last house in Kentucky on Gaines Way. We bought an unfinished home with six acres of five-foot-high grass and a pond with a dam that was covered in building debris from the original owner who dumped it there, but it never deterred us from our dream. We spent the next six years putting it back together and trying to finish it. The entry stairs and the handrail had been torn out, but we found enough of the original pieces scattered about the house to get it put back together. The master bath was torn apart with plumbing sticking out of the floor and the toilet setting in the shower.

I remember having to take apart the master spa tub since it was setting crooked, only to find that the scrap boards were left underneath it, causing it to be out of level. The framework was undersized and incomplete, so I had to rebuild it as well. Once again, I found enough remaining ceramic tile to finish covering the newly built frame around the spa as well. Before being able to install the new kitchen cabinets, I had to rework the raised floor to make more space for the dining table and had to rework the oak floors to make it all match.

I could hear the words "Work never killed nobody" as I spent over six weeks clearing the six acres of five-foot-tall grass, only to discover various piles of rubble and rock that had to be removed. Once I was down to the rehab of the pond dam, I used the help of an excavation company to dig a twenty-by-twenty-foot-deep hole to deposit the dug-up, abandoned building materials, then had them rebuild the dam with an overflow that it was missing as well. Once it was done, I spent the next three months removing field stones from the dam and surrounding yard, which led to many, many trailer loads of rock being hauled to the creek bed on our property as well. In order to have adequate room for all the equipment to maintain the six acres properly, I had a thirty-six-by-forty-eight-foot barn with three garage stalls and an eighteen-by-thirty-six-foot shop built, along with filling in the driveway around it.

Back inside the house, I finished rearranging basement walls to install a theatre room, and in the process, I found the insulation missing to the floor joists of the first floor, so I had to take down four feet of the perimeter ceiling that had been installed to put in the needed insulation. After completing the theatre room walls and insulating the basement ceiling, I repurposed the original kitchen cabinets to make a kitchen area in the basement, using the countertop and sink from the kitchen cabinets upstairs to finish it.

We now had a mostly finished house that we could raise our four kids in. I had those moments of frustration, like stepping on a stovetop while installing a new kitchen exhaust, but mostly felt the sense of pride of a job well done as we saw areas of our home come together, and then had many great memories after, like birthdays, graduations, wedding showers, baby showers, Thanksgiving dinners, and Christmas mornings.

As I further think of my dad's words, I never realized that the perseverance and self-motivation would lead to moments of pride, happiness, triumph, and ultimately rejuvenation or new motivation to keep on going.

Life lesson: It makes sense now how these words helped my dad and myself push through, for it's not the work that keeps you from success, but the results and satisfaction that you receive at the end that drive you on to success.

It's not about the destination but the journey, they say, especially if you make the time, as I now can stop and look around at what we have accomplished. I was so focused on making a home for my wife and four kids that I lost track of the quantity of work it was taking. At the same time, the individual efforts of work never bothered me, for dad's word were playing in the back of my mind as I was working through each task. I recognized the value of each step from my continuous improvement training from the Japanese at Toyota.

Continuous improvement is not about quantum leaps or major innovation in a single step, but all about small baby steps of repeated improvements. The Japanese culture for continuous improvement is based in agriculture, for they too were based around being farmers. The Japanese appreciate developing things in a manual method so they can find the most efficient methods first before automating it. This approach requires lots of manual labor at first, so it takes the perseverance and self-motivation that comes from my dad's words. It is this methodology or belief that has kept me happy at Toyota. It so meshes with how my dad raised me.

These same principles are the ones that allow Toyota to maintain its relationships with suppliers. Toyota is committed to work with its suppliers, not only teaching them, but demonstrate continuous improvement as well. It is this philosophy that easily convinced me to provide six team members to work with a seat supplier who was struggling to meet production. As a company, we spent several months working side by side in the dead of winter in an unheated parts warehouse to not only create new and improved processes but to also sort through parts that were lost in piles of orders. They were not just inside the warehouse but also in dozens of tractor trailers at a local airport. We found new parts so dated that the part numbers were now obsolete and no longer useful for production.

As a culture, we never gave up working with a supplier. It required the perseverance and even self-motivation of my dad's words to push through and help teach a supplier outside our culture these simple values, to have the resolve to improve their operations. This takes me back to my earlier thought of "How do you get someone motivated to do work when they have never experienced the value of it themselves?" Similar to the continuous improvement that we demonstrated to our suppliers, I believe you need to show someone that work never killed nobody by displaying perseverance and self-motivation. In that effort, initially one must have their own self-motivation and perseverance, for the one following you may not be much help in supporting the work at first. A person teaching the value of work may feel most of the burden and need the value of my dad's words to push through.

Life lesson: The key to getting the student to realize work is worth it is to make sure they see

the incremental gains or improvements from their work.

I believe the Japanese realized the need to show improvement from their culture of farming, and that's why the continuous improvement methodology has the cycle of plan, do, check, act. Like the four seasons of farming, the key to a successful harvest in the fall starts with the preparation or planning done in the offseason. This planning evolves with studying and analyzing what we have done or results from the past season. In the study, we compare what we intended to do (our plan) versus our received results (our actual). The key in this study is to realize the bad results in order to determine what did not work and its root cause for not succeeding. Then we need to consider the good results to determine what did work and, more importantly, what the keys are to good results. This allows us to minimize the efforts to achieve those results and eliminate wasted effort, or *muda*, as it known in the Toyota production system.

This methodology is the key to Toyota's continual improvement and success as a company. By focusing on both bad and good results with an intention to learn, a person can see the value from their effort. I believe seeking out periodic results from our work is key to showing the value of my dad's ideals. It also helps to answer how to get someone to believe in this life lesson when, from their perspective, they have never received value from hard work.

Many people perceive failure as bad, but if one takes the approach that is just a bad result, or more importantly, a no-good result, then they have the opportunity to learn from it. As they try again and see some things improve, they can look for the lessons from the no-good and good results, then adjust again. Ultimately, they will get to their intended results. I believe this process takes place for the farmer as well when they realize which crops do better in their fields; which equipment does a better job to plow, seed, or harvest; which process produces more bushels at harvest; or which harvest provides the greatest good to allow them to sustain their farm as a business.

I believe a person needs to start with the mindset of "Work never killed nobody" to get started with self-motivation, and to maintain perseverance, they need to stop and measure their results so they can realize the value they have created. As I studied successful people, whether it's Walt Disney, Henry Ford, or even Thomas Edison, I realize these folks were not afraid to work and not afraid to fail or have a no-good result. They all had the resolve or perseverance to carry on with their work. In my family, this resolve was known as "grit," which has both self-motivation and perseverance as ingredients.

I realize now that this grit comes from one's willingness to accept what is perceived as both no-good and good results. For many, work is not worth it, but I believe it's their perception from a no-good result, which truly is based on a perspective.

> **Life lesson: I realize that my dad's words was intended to instill grit or resolve to carry on in order to be successful in life, whether it's for yourself, your family, or for someone else.**

Once you deeply understand the value of these words, I believe you will only be driven more to carry on where most would tend to give up. Ironically, I realize this was most likely put into my mind not only by my dad and his daily actions but also by the words from the "Uncommon Man" poem I received from National Junior Honor Society: "One who seeks opportunity, takes the calculated risk, to dream and build, to fail and succeed, to stand proud and enjoy the benefit of my creations."

I realize how I utilized this during my work in real estate. I had studied successful entrepreneurs in real estate prior to making my first strategic step into a real estate deal. I spent the first year and a half hearing "no" for financing, but along the way, I learned the market in northern Kentucky was tied up by a select group. This drove a need to study similar housing to learn the potential upside in rents, so that ultimately, I would have a more compelling story. In fact, I learned the story so well that I received my first "yes" from a local bank vice president who I cold-called via a walk-in to the bank, not even having my PowerPoint to present at the time.

Furthermore, as I worked on this first property with my wife, I recall those moments of needing my dad's words to keep me going, for three of the eleven units needed some major rehabs. The previous owner left these units empty for over seven years, as I learned from the existing tenants. These revelations came about not only while we were committed to rehabbing but also committed to responding at the same time to the existing tenant repairs, which did seem overwhelming at times. One unit had to be exterminated multiple times and sealed off before we could even go in and throw out the furniture and trash left behind.

As we started to fill all the units, we were able to use the improved cash flow to begin rehabbing the exterior. We replaced single pane windows from the 1960s with sealed thermal-pane glass, and as we did this, we noticed we could then reduce the energy needed from the central boiler. That lowered our utility expense and increased our cash flow so we could do even more capital improvements that, in turn, allowed us to charge more rent for the improved units. At the time, we did not yet realize the value of our work until it was time to prepare our story for the next deal. It was in the preparation of our story that I recognized not only the value we created from our work but also the bad and good results.

The bad was the lost opportunity in income due to the time to do the rehabs ourselves, while the good was really understanding which changes were necessary to make an impact on what new tenants were willing to pay for. We realized that good, functioning kitchen cabinets with a coat of paint in today's color trends, like a dark brown, were just as impactful as new kitchen cabinets, especially if we replaced the 1960s countertops with today's designs and colors that mixed well with the dark-brown paint of the cabinets. Just from the similar Toyota process of "plan, do, check, act," I recognized the work that made bad results, like buying new kitchen cabinets that cost more money with the same impact as a lower-cost approach of just painting the old kitchen cabinets versus the good results, like the impact of a new countertop and sink.

With some lessons learned and the value we received from our first property and a great story to close the deal, we embarked on a larger property, where thirteen of thirty-one units needed major rehabs as well as three buildings that needed new roofs. As we drove on with my dad's words, we were fueled with our lessons learned from our first investment property. We began to purchase labor to support us in these major rehabs, which took our six-month cycle time for major rehabs down to three months and also allowed us to take our one-to three-month turns down to one month.

At the same time of the unit rehab, we committed to replace the similar 1960s single-pane windows with thermal glass due to what we had learned about the energy savings and utility bills on the central boiler. One thing that we did differently on our second property was to make time along the way of our work to analyze the results—

both bad and good—which helped us to maintain our efforts and live out my dad's words. Through this so-called continuous improvement process of our own, we realized value in putting laminate floors in the living room with a tile entry so that they weathered foot traffic well, while the carpet was quick, cheap, and quieted down the bedroom spaces, making the tenants happier. We realized the bad results of shower enclosures, which were easily broken, versus the resilience of the more expensive tile-installed bathrooms. It was fascinating to learn that our $2,800 per unit rehab done by our own labor that was now $5,700 per unit with purchased labor, but it was easily recovered in the three extra months of rent created by the reduced cycle time of unit rehab.

At the same time, more newly rehabbed units increased the value of the property and justified increased rent, even for existing tenants. Justification was reinforced as we improved the common areas of the buildings, such as the entry walls, halls, and laundry rooms with the additional income from the increased rents of the rehabbed and existing units as the property improved. In the units with existing tenants, we began to pull ahead the replacements of the 1960s single-pane windows with the thermal-pane glass so that the existing tenants could see the value in paying more rent as well.

It was interesting as well to see our impact on the tenants themselves as we displayed my dad's words of "Work never killed nobody." We noticed our tenants doing more for themselves by taking better care of their units and the common areas as they picked up their trash and other items they dropped, whether it was in the hall, laundry room, or even the parking lots. Furthermore, the tenants changed their expectations of the other tenants around them, as they would call us to let us know if someone had left trash in a common area or had mistreated or broken something. As I look back on the impact we had on the second property, I'm so honored that Dad's words were passed on not only to ourselves as a family but also to our tenants and most likely their families too as things improved and were seen as better.

These successes from those first two properties built in the 1960s led to us having the ability to sell them and acquire a similar-sized property that was twenty years newer. Suddenly, it seemed that my dad's words led to a place where there were no longer major rehabs due to units left in a disgusting situation. The new property rehabs were now changed to upgrades for many of the units. They were larger spaces with two bedrooms for small families, where the parents were making a decent income. Again, using our lessons learned from our second property, we started with purchased labor and installed laminate flooring and tile for the high-traffic areas.

Recognizing the need to increase our checking of results, both bad and good, we recognized that new-looking kitchens needed the addition of new appliances. We found that the new look was achieved whether we installed stainless steel or black appliances, but the black appliances were usually much cheaper and easier to clean up when a tenant vacated the unit. As we now were able to charge rent at the higher end of the range for the area, we realized the need to clean the common areas more often, so we also purchased labor to maintain the halls, parking lot, and the surrounding yard more frequently.

Once again, as we improved the property, even the existing tenants began to take better care of things in their units and in the common areas. In fact, we started to have existing tenants ask for their units to be upgraded. At first, it started with just painting their walls, then they wanted us back in to replace the floors. We even had the same tenants come back and want an entire kitchen upgrade, and they were willing to pay more again to move into a newly upgraded unit. Suddenly, our display of "Work never killed nobody" had tenants wanting us to work for them, even if it meant us charging them more rent.

It is interesting to then realize that those tenants who wanted upgrades and would pay more rent were in the end ultimately learning my dad's lesson. It was exciting to see our work in real estate blossom from working to just make units rentable, to expand to make units that provided more value to our tenants. They were proud to rent the units and wanted the improvements, even if it meant spending more money.

Life lesson: By our willingness to work, we had taught strangers the value of work even though many had not been people who saw a need for self-motivation and perseverance.

My dad's words and actions had now not only been passed on to my family and friends but also to people whom we were working for.

As work stabilized on our third property, I began to focus back to our own property on Gaines Way. Similar to our investment properties, Gaines Way was no longer a major rehab like the first six years there. Gaines Way was now a home that needed upgrades. With the help of my son-in-law, we were able to install new floors in the basement and even install a new full bath to complement the previously installed theatre room and kitchen area.

We got help as well to install a new enclosed patio room and even an enlarged deck to connect the patio room to the existing porch that allowed an amazing view of our now-beautiful pond, all of which achieved from the work of those initial six years of our own labor. To finish out the look at the rear of the house, I built a pergola with a clear-glass roof that would eventually lead to a new slab of concrete and a newly installed swim spa on top of it. In addition, I got help to rework the stone to the basement door, install new stone to the area of the basement walls next to it, and finally, a new concrete slab at the entrance to the basement door. To complete the look at the front of the house, I installed the stone at the exposed areas of the foundation prior to having a new sidewalk poured to the front door.

After sixteen years in our Gaines Way house, the value from my dad's words clearly paid off. The incomplete house with overgrown grass and missing stairs and master bath was now a beautiful four-bedroom, four-bath home with a beautiful view of woods and pond. As I stood on that front porch again like I did with my dad in 2006 when I first looked at the property, I could hear his words, "Well, if you keep doing what you have been doing, then you're going to keep getting what you have been getting," and now wondered what if I had not taken the step to be "uncommon" and prescribed to the notion of "Work never killed nobody."

I realized, like many others who struggle to be successful, that I would not be standing on the front porch of an amazingly beautiful home, or more exactly, an estate without living on ,y dad's words on work.

At that moment, I deeply recognized the value of my dad's words and wondered how much he knew his words were going to impact myself, my family, my friends, and even strangers with the results that I would create from those by simply "resolving to carry on." Thanks, Dad!

IT TAKES MONEY TO MAKE MONEY

My dad was born in 1929, so it was surprising to hear him say, "It takes money to make money." But I knew he meant it from a business viewpoint. He told me many times that you can't be afraid to spend money, for you're never going to make money that way. He grew up a farmer but knew the value of money as an entrepreneur, and that's why I know he loved having our company, the BJC Painting and Construction Maintenance. The farmer side of him always expensed things sparingly. He kept things and used them forever, if possible. This mindset meshed well with my life at Toyota, where the Japanese people, living on an island with limited resources and many of them farmers, were very much about making an asset last forever.

It was interesting to watch him clean paintbrushes and wrap them in newspaper to keep the bristles straight, change his own oil, pack his own wheel bearings, change his own spark plugs, and sharpen his own lawn mower blades. Plus, he would fix, if possible, anything that was found broken around the house even if it was discovered as we worked on a job such as a broken or loose handrail.

In contrast, he always purchased the best paintbrushes and always added E-B Emulsa Bond to our paint to ensure that our customer's paint job was going to stick, even though many times, the existing surface could have been painted without the Emulsa Bond. I remember Dad going to JCPenney to make sure he had nice shoes and dress pants for Sunday church and dinner. The idea of making sure you bought and used good things also matched well with my Toyota culture, for the Japanese also spared no expense to buy good equipment but, like my dad, only bought what they needed—no extra frills, just good quality, and only the quantity needed to be successful. As I have reflected on my life in real estate, I now see how his simple lesson made so much sense.

My first recognition in real estate investment of the life lesson "It takes money to make money" was in our first multiunit building. After learning from the existing tenants that three of the eleven units had not been rented in over seven years, I realized the previous owner thought he could not make enough money if he had to make major capital investments. The funny part was he was losing out on $1,200 per month rent for the last seven years, which is a cash flow loss of over $100,000. Those rehabs cost us $2,800 per unit so we were paid back in five months. I had been taught by successful real estate investors to focus on cash flow, do the math, and do the right thing.

> **Life lesson: I began to realize my dad's words and his further explanation to not be afraid to spend money to make money. It not only made more sense now, but I could actually use basic math to make sure the improvement works out for cash flow.**

I realize his words about not being afraid to spend money were so important to be willing to consider even spending money but also to do the math so you know the outcome or, more importantly, the benefit. As I consider why my dad was not afraid to spend money in a smart way, I believe this thinking had to come from his life lesson of being born at the start of the Great Depression. I had asked him what growing up in the Great Depression was like, and his biggest recollection was the family getting a bag of oranges for Christmas, which were expensive at the time since no one typically saw them the rest of the year. I now imagine that growing up without money could be the reason my dad was not afraid to spend it on the right things. He had experienced life without money and understood life still goes on anyway. At the same time, my dad always said you should keep a couple thousand in the bank for a rainy day, which were the words of his dad, my grandpa Ogle Glenn, and it makes sense now more than ever as his first son was born just two months into the greatest economic turmoil of the twentieth century, which was truly a rainy day that lasted till 1939.

As I reflect to my dad buying me a Toro power-driven lawn mower for my sixth birthday, I realize his commitment to the words "It takes money to make money," for he bought an expensive, reliable brand, with a necessary option for a six-year-old boy to be successfully mowing lawns. His own mower was a simple push type, which he used to assist me in mowing several lawns at a time. He could have bought a simple push mower for me too, but I believe he knew the cost of success for his six-year-old little man who was mowing lawns.

Even though he let me buy my own first car at the age of fifteen—a 1967 C10 Chevrolet pickup truck—with savings from my paper route, I realized he wanted to make sure I had a safe, reliable car for college when he bought me a used 1983 Chevrolet Monte Carlo LS, which was only two years old, for high school graduation. I believe that him allowing me to have the truck first taught me the value of money, and needing to fix it up also taught me how to work and maintain vehicles.

In contrast, I believe my dad knew the value of a college education in engineering, and he spent the money on a vehicle that he knew would get me there and back each semester. To further make note of my dad's recognition of a college education, I learned five years later that my first job as an engineer paid an annual salary that was more than the combined salary of my parents that year. I was in shock as I helped my parents with their taxes, but I never said a word. I was fighting back the tears of pride and love for two parents who made sure I had what I needed. It was another clear moment of my dad's life lesson, and he clearly showed me that—not just with the Monte Carlo my senior year of high school, but also at six years old when he bought a Toro power-driven mower to mow lawns to make money myself.

As I read Napoleon Hill's *Think and Grow Rich*, I wondered if my dad had the same sense to envision the amount of money he needed and put it into memory so he would recognize it and act upon it when it came about. I watched him make plans and figures on notebooks, whether it was for his future woodshop, carport, new painting job, or even vacation. I remember him having our vacation money in traveler's checks since I went with my mom to AAA to buy them. I never recall my dad worrying about having money. Even when my mom shared her concern at times, my dad would always say, "I'm not worried about the money. If I need to, I will go make some more or find it somehow." These words made me recognize how powerful an experience, in a positive way, it was for my dad to grow up in the Great Depression. My life lessons from watching him make plans on notebooks was learning more of the math from successful real estate investors about things like NOI (net operating income) and cap rate (NOI as a percentage of capital investment). I recognize "Doing the math" and "It takes money to make money" helped me to successfully rebuild our second real estate investment. Similar to our first investment, the owner had not wanted to spend any capital since it took away from his NOI. The funny part was he had lost two of three units on the third floor of the building due to the leaking roof, which was creating a loss of more than $1,800 per month in rent. In addition, I could see that water infiltration was making its way to the second and first floors in places. We added the installation of a new roof to the purchase of the building and placed it in escrow, which the owner was happy to do get us to buy his three buildings. I remember talking to the owner at closing about the roof and remember him saying, "I hate to spend the money, but I know it needs to get done."

It truly made my head hurt and actually sad for the previous owner to not have my dad's life lesson, for he had not only lost out on the income from those two units, but we soon realized as we studied the rent roll more closely that thirteen of the thirty-one units in the three buildings were either vacant due to unrepaired kitchens or bathrooms, broken windows, bad ceilings, leaking foundations. Similar to the first investment, two units on the first floor had been left in studs from water damage that had happened over ten years earlier, per the existing tenants.

We focused at first on simpler units, where we could maintain the cabinets and replace countertops. Also, we found that the floors below were beautiful three-quarter-inch oaks that could be sanded and stained in many cases, which was better than our plan for vinyl laminate in high-traffic areas. It was interesting as well to learn that the previous owner, who didn't want to spend money, had overfilled two large storage rooms and all the thirteen vacant units with paint, hardware, supplies, and various replacement parts that allowed us to do most of all the unit repairs over the eight years that we owned the property and also provided a third of the parts and supplies to do the rehabs on the thirteen units as well.

The previous owner, who had owned it for over thirty years, let others manage and maintain it so he had not realized how many parts and supplies were purchased and not used, for they were not kept together in one place. Even funnier was the fact that a maintenance guy who worked on the building for over twenty years made one of the rooms a perfect general store, with several shelves over twenty feet long with easy-to-pull-out parts bins that could be labeled.

As we completed the vacant thirteen units, we would first move the leftover supplies and parts to the next rehab unit, especially if those parts and supplies were clearly needed as part of the work. In addition, if the leftover parts and supplies were not needed for the next rehab, then I began to take them to the well-established storage room, putting them in the same parts bin if possible. As I gathered more leftover parts and supplies and saw the magnitude of money spent but not used, I realized a valuable lesson.

> **Life lesson: You must spend money to make money, but also need to pay attention to what you have and what you are getting; otherwise, you are wasting money—that money is now not making you money.**

This was a key to my dad's life lesson, with an added clause of "as long as the money spent is for something that is actually invested in something that is making money itself."

As I ponder the key lesson, I realize this is why the wealthy are wealthy. They focus first on making money make money versus making money to spend money, which is what myself and so many others do by going to work, then coming home to spend it on the things we want to enjoy. I believe this is the single most valuable enhancement that I learned from successful real estate investors and from studying folks like Napoleon Hill and Wallace D. Wattles. I'm now wondering if there might be a good math formula that shows this approach. I believe there is something better than the typical "15 to 20 percent of income should be used for savings," which is only setting money aside to earn only 1 to 2-percent interest, which does not make a real impact on what's been saved.

I now realize that putting that money into an investment is a real key to what my dad's words meant. A good investment is one that should make 8 to 9-percent interest on your money. This is what is known as cap rate to real investors. I think the fundamental flaw with the two owners that we purchased from was their inability to look beyond ROI (return on investment) or cap rate or interest on their money. When you only focus on ROI in real estate, you lose the ability to see that your money is degrading in its ability to make money for the actual property, and it starts to lose value. As those real estate units become dated or worn, the value of your rent begins to peak and ultimately declines as compared to the rest of the market. Over time, what appears as a process of making money while expenses are low suddenly starts to become negative, especially when those units not only become worn or dated but also finally become vacant as they are in a state of disrepair that makes them uninhabitable. That was the case with the ones we found with water damage from the roof or the broken fixtures in the kitchens and bathrooms.

It takes discipline and a fine balance to realize the ultimate benefit of my dad's words. If you focus too much on making money, or ROI, then you risk the chance of it losing value to produce over time.

> **Life lesson: If you don't focus on spending money to see that it's being utilized effectively, you may find it's being wasted, like how we found with parts and supplies sitting idle versus being used to repair and rehab units.**

As I have realized these lessons on the discipline and focus that is required for my dad's ways, I have found real-world examples of successful people who have utilized this approach to money. One of my favorite engineers, or *Imagineers* as he himself coined, is Walt Disney. I have been fascinated by the magic he created in his theme parks and animations. As I have studied his career, I realized that his ideas, like a theme park, take a lot of money to create. A typical new ride at a Disney theme park costs around $120 million dollars. On top of the capital investment, these rides require the same level of maintenance as an elevator. That's finally how the government classified them, for they are typically carrying people in them like an elevator does.

I began to wonder about the level of capital required to build and maintain a theme park. How do you even begin the cycle of "It takes money to make money?" In this type of situation, one of Walt's key points to his cast members is to "Remember this all began with a mouse." Of course, that mouse was Mickey Mouse. First, Walt's saying told me, "Don't forget where you came from" or "Pay attention to the fundamentals," which parallels the need to focus on where you are spending money to make money. As I studied Walt, his focus in developing theme parks was incredible. Walt started with a story or focus or purpose using storyboards to hone not just the ride highlights but, more importantly, what the guest would walk away with in their hearts and minds. I learned that the story helped his brother Roy sell the concept to bankers and investors to work on "finding the money," as my dad would say to my mom.

Next, Walt would further his focus by developing scaled models of the park rides, and even the space between them, in detail. Walt would then use motor-driven cameras to walk through the model as if a guest to confirm the that story was not only delivered but also in a way that had the right perspective, the right lighting, and the right amenities to ensure the guest experience, such as restrooms, food, drinks, and souvenirs.

Parallel to Walt's efforts, his brother Roy would use the details of Walt's stories to develop advertising and marketing. The marketing Roy did was not just in making the story gain momentum and excitement but also in marketing with Walt Disney exclusive products that are sold before, during, and after the release of Walt's rides. I believe it took Roy believing in Walt's visions to have the courage to chase down the money, and in contrast, it took the relentless focus of Walt to perfect the story and everything around it. It took Roy's commitment of "It takes money to make money" to not get caught up in the ROI from the last Walt project and not take the risk of spending money on the next one. At the same time, it is clear that Walt worked on every detail, so using the money effectively and not wasting it was important, which is in line with my own personal reflections of learning as we worked in real estate. I believe that Walt and Roy together embodied the necessary qualities that really ensure that my dad's words are successful.

The amazing part as well is that Roy made sure that his and Walt's wisdom is carried on as the Walt Disney company brings in new team members. The company raises them up through the organization with Walt's foundation of the Imagineering team that sticks to the details of making the story and focus to make sure each ride and even animation has perfect details to match and support the story.

> **Life lesson: The Disney brothers helped me realize that "Focus to spend wisely" and "Not just focusing on ROI" are the keys to success with "It takes money to make money."**

As I studied another successful person, Powell Crosley Jr., I began to see similar approaches to the Disney brothers. Powell Jr. was an amazing engineer and idea guy like Walt Disney. Powell really focused on the engineering side of things as he created designs that could be broken down into an assembly line, which was in line with his love of the automobile. Powell also understood the marketing side of things, as he not only used names like *Roamio* for his after-market radios and *Shelvadoor* for his line of refrigerators, which was the first time shelves were built into doors. He made choices based on needs he saw from a consumer perspective and made things universal enough with patent rights so they could be used by other manufacturers for a price.

Parallel to Powell's efforts, his brother Lewis made sure the finances were in order to support the business and ensure the funding was available to do the heavy lifting of research and development, plus support the creation of equipment to make the design into a real product.

The downside of the Crosley Brothers empire was that they did not develop their wisdom into a philosophy that could be made into a long-term company culture, like the Disney brothers did. Now the Crosley company is lost, except for seeing the name on retro media products like vinyl record players, but most likely, no one who purchases them realizes that the name was on radios, cars, and appliances. The company had even created the most powerful radio station ever, the 500,000-watt WLW.

I would imagine people don't realize that soap operas and public advertising on radio and TV were also the creations of the Crosley empire and are still part of mainstream media today. I realize with these life lessons, reflections, and sharing how different the ending of legacy becomes and how dependent it is on sharing your wisdom.

Life lesson: To ensure a legacy remains from my dad's words, it is most important to share your wisdom so that it lives beyond yourself and thus becomes bigger than yourself.

As I ponder over this idea of legacy, I suddenly realize how my dad left me his own legacy by constantly sharing and living his life lessons in front of me. In contrast, by comparing the Disney brothers and the Crosley brothers, I truly realize how blessed I am in being able to share my life lesson from my dad and those I've studied, whether in person or through their biographies.

Life lesson: My choice of the words *No Regrets* was not only intentional but also right in the fact that I don't want to walk out of this world without sharing the wonderful wisdom I have gained, even if it's only words that my children take in and do something spectacular with them in their own right.

As an engineer at Toyota focused to implement capital improvements for new model changes, it is obvious that the approach of "It takes money to make money" is a vital one. It is the process of investing capital that ensures our products evolve and keep the interest of our customers. Similar to the Disney and Crosley brothers, the process of capital improvement starts with details. These details form into plans that are the story or purpose of the capital investment. Working in multiple areas in production engineering, I have been blessed to see and work in assembly plants, unit plants, and the facilities for those plants.

Planning at Toyota is that "focus" mentioned earlier that makes sure we use the money well or efficiently. With the image of the next vehicle being clear, our focus begins by studying the design needed for a new vehicle, then comparing the new design to the existing design for the currently-produced vehicle. Once design differences are understood, then it is time to study the process that turns that design into manufacturable steps that combine tools, people, and automation. It has been interesting to see the impact of people on the focus required to work in the various areas of manufacturing. In assembly, the process people are at the center, especially since part variation is high and requires human-level intelligence to confirm the color, proper orientation, and fit, particularly since some parts are optional based on customer preference. The focus needed in a people-centric process is one that does not only consider manufacturability but also ensure good ergonomics and incorporate double checks to minimize burden on the human as they deal with variation each and every minute to meet production needs.

The unit process is machine- or automation-centric, since part variation is replaced with processes that have a high level of accuracy. To ensure not only manufacturability but also the high quality of machined part, the focus must ensure clear data and clear targets for part variation so the stack up does not create functional issues. Also required is the ability to measure consistently, including a way for humans to confirm the quality of the things measured.

In facilities, the process is both people- and machine-centric since the process size or space is huge. The focus in facilities starts with standards to minimize variation in order to more easily manage the size of the spaces or process. The standards allow people in facilities to ensure reliability needed, especially in the form of utilities that allow the assembly and unit processes to run by providing a reliable machine. As can be seen by the variation in a vehicle production process, the focus must consider the use of man and machine, which is determined by the method we choose to manufacture the product.

In a large organization like the ones needed to manufacture complex products like an automobile, it is easy to be siloed as a group focuses on their unique area like design, manufacturing, logistics, sales, or marketing. This type of large organization makes it possible to lose sight of the bigger goal of its product. In addition to the focus struggles of a large organization, it becomes inherent that someone must minimize the risk of too much money being spent just due to the expansiveness of a project. As that group begins to minimize or control the money of each group, the development of an area begins to get minimized in the name of "managing cost" to ensure the ROI for the product.

I have recognized that managing cost inherent in a large organization starts to take away from my dad's words, "It takes money to make money." These large organizations start to impact the group's ability to try to develop new ideas and lower their desire to even try to innovate their area. The worry over ROI in a large organization begins to look similar to those previous owners of real estate who

I purchased from, who started to minimize expense in the name of ROI, which ultimately led to their product, buildings, and units to lose value.

Life lesson: This same issue, concern for ROI, starts to impact the product of large organizations for the product starts to lose its value to the customer, as each group begins to minimize innovation as they support the effort of reducing cost.

In contrast, I have noticed large organizations who still do well to innovate. One of the most popular large organizations that is expected and known for innovation is Apple. As I have studied Apple's founder, Steve Jobs, I recognize that he combined the focus of a product that delivered innovation with a standard of quality without regard to cost. Steve made up for cost by demanding a price from the customer that covered the upfront investment and the investment to manufacture it.

The key that Steve Jobs used was the marketing. Steve built excitement and a thirst for new technology. Building a following of customers who not only wanted but also somehow needed the new iPhone or iPad because the new features were superior to the previous ones. I recognize that the retail cost for an Apple product was approached completely the opposite way from what I have seen in most large manufacturing organizations. For Apple, the retail price is derived once the product is completed based on the required development costs, manufacturing costs, and profit needed to sustain the company as well as future development. For most large manufacturing organizations, the sales group determines a reasonable retail cost or forecast, to which the financial controls group adds a standard profit margin, then uses historical data to define the cost typically spent in each area of design, manufacturing, logistics, sales, and marketing. That retail cost for each product is now broken into area costs, then multiplied by a forecasted sales volume for the model life, which then derives the capital investment that can be spent. The struggle with the latter approach is that the cost is based on history of actual costs, which most likely is based on the historical costs that were controlled, and therefore, innovation was stifled.

This approach leads to an inherent minimization of innovation while at the same time, these same organizations advertise the need for, and the culture of, innovation. It takes a bold leader like Steve Jobs to establish a need that a customer is willing to place a high value on. Again, it's similar to what I saw in real estate when new tenants were willing to pay higher rent for a unit that to them is new and built with good amenities that make it acceptable to pay for what is perceived as a higher value.

As I compare my life lessons to my dad's words, "You have to spend money to make money," I recognize that my original impression was not as accurate as I thought. My original thought was that bold moves were what spending money to make money was all about. In simpler terms, bold moves simply involve taking risks. As I have learned by watching my dad with his own company, as well as studying the Disney, Crosley, and Apple companies, it is more specifically a calculated risk. The calculated part is the focus during a so-called planning phase, or prior to the kickoff of actually working on the creation itself.

This focus during the planning phase is to make clear the purpose and forecasted costs to meet the purpose. When the cost is accepted, it is important for the project leader to make sure the team does not deviate from the purpose and choose the most efficient way to meet that purpose. Walt was the project leader at Walt Disney, Powell was the project leader at Crosley, and Steve was the project leader at Apple. The key for sustainability of this is to have the process of planning well-documented, as has been done at both Walt Disney and Apple. This can be seen by the continued delivery of new projects or technology that the customers keep coming back for, even when it requires a higher price to purchase those goods or services than the previous ones.

In addition to focus, a new project takes leadership commitment to the project's purpose and value to ensure that it does not get lost to impacting current ROI. Roy was the project champion at Walt Disney, Lewis was the project champion at Crosley, and Steve was the project champion at Apple. The key for sustainability of this is to have the vision and mission clear and well-documented in the leadership training and succession planning to make sure the future leadership has the right mindset to sustain the culture of the company. As I think about this from my training at the Project Management Institute, this commitment documentation is what is known in the industry as a project charter.

As can be seen from my reflections, my dad's words have a lot more complexity to them as they are put into practice. Watching him successfully run a company of his own for over eleven years, I imagine he truly understood those complexities. It's interesting as well how the previously mentioned life lessons, such as "You can do anything you want to if you put your mind to it," really support the focus needed for planning and the needed focus during implementation to ensure the purpose is maintained and realized.

Similarly, the life lesson of helping others really supports the notion today called "servant leadership," which ensures buy-in and commitment from the team, along with the focus needed to ensure that the best way is found to ensure quality while minimizing costs. The life lesson of taking the day off supports our ability to focus by providing us the space to ponder and refine the purpose by taking the time to make sure the plan follows and, more importantly, supports the vision intended. The space gained from taking the day off lets you develop and consider options so that you can ensure the most effective and efficient plan is made to use the money spent wisely.

The life lesson "Work is life, so get used to it" is important in the development of the plan because, as stated previously, "Work equals life" is all about adding value, which will lead to a plan that is the most effective and efficient. The life lesson also means that it is necessary to provide value to myself and others. As you're working through the plan, it is necessary to have the life lesson "Work never killed nobody" to drive us with self-motivation and "perseverance to stay focused on being effective and efficient while making sure the purpose is achieved.

I share these correlations between the life lessons so that one can begin to realize the value in understanding all of them as well as the value in using them together to ensure success, whether it be personal like being physically fit, completing a home project for yourself or family, or for your career, like completing a capital project.

It takes time and repetition to not only understand the words but also to realize the ancillary values and necessary deeper meanings and practices to ensure that the actions intended from these words will lead to success. I can imagine my dad pondering all these things, whether under the stars at night plowing the fields in southern Ohio, or in the sun at Myrtle Beach while soaking in the sound of the ocean waves.

It makes sense that a farmer uses words that are simple and practical, but profoundly necessary, just like the process of farming itself. In farming, the same basic steps are used, but the harvest rests on the ability to do the right things at the right time, as well as to prepare and wait, but act quickly when the time is right.

IF YOU KEEP DOING WHAT YOU'VE BEEN DOING, THEN YOU'LL KEEP GETTING WHAT YOU'VE BEEN GETTING

As I was getting to my early forties, I felt myself in a relentless pursuit of my life purpose. I constantly had this notion of "It's halftime." Like a football game, at halftime, the team is in the locker room pouring over the first-half stats, looking for the good points and trying to figure out how get better from their mistakes.

I had been in two groups in Toyota Production Engineering and worked on projects in eleven of the thirteen sites in North America, which covers the US, Canada, and Mexico. I had survived the move from Ohio to Michigan to Kentucky, where I started in the assembly group and suddenly was on my own with a contract staff member to finish up the 1997 model Sienna in Georgetown, Kentucky. All the assembly members had joined in Michigan, which was their home, and they were not interested in moving to Kentucky. The long hours spent to not only finish up the project at winter shutdown but also close out the punch list made those nine months seem like nine years. During that same period, major life events were happening—my wife was pregnant with our second daughter, then she was hospitalized from dehydration and struggled with her health until she delivered the baby. My wife finally moved us from Michigan to Kentucky while our second daughter was only six weeks old. At the same time, I signed us up to buy a newly built home in Kentucky, which led us not only to modify its design to meet our needs but required us to make all the exterior and interior design decisions in one day. It was my wife's only chance, since we were in Kentucky on a Toyota site visit that had been arranged for new families moving there to work at the new North American Headquarters in Erlanger, Kentucky.

We started in an apartment in Kentucky with our newborn daughter as they finished our house. We had all our things in storage, so we rented furniture for our apartment. We got to enjoy the Christmas of 1996 in our New Kentucky home, which was amazing. We loved our new place, and so did our daughters. I was promoted to manager the following year and given responsibility to develop the new site in Princeton, Indiana, which took up the next three years of my life. As my wife and two daughters started settling into their new home, I was back and forth across Interstate 64 every week to Indiana, as well as having regular trips to Toyota offices in Japan to learn. My life was full between a full-time traveling job and two little girls who were in dance, soccer, and all things kids do.

Six years later, my youngest daughter became sick on the road with our family as she was getting ready to start kindergarten. We found out at her school health check that she had early onset scoliosis, which was not the diagnosis we expected. Life continued for her and us with six month check-ups and the addition of a back brace, or "shield," as she called it.

A year later, I was moved unexpectedly from assembly to powertrain, and the next four years involved more regular trips to Japan. As I turned forty in 2007, I was told by the company leadership that I had to decide between being a general manager or a dad, for I could not do both. This really led to that halftime feeling I had mentioned. At that moment in my mental locker room, I recognized that I had been blessed in my career at Toyota, for I had gained a lot of responsibility. On the other hand, the success at Toyota came at a price—long hours, driving at times thirteen hours a day to make an eight-hour day in Huntsville, Alabama, then be home for an early morning school event, then back to Alabama. I never complained about that in front of the girls, but I sure felt I missed out on the smaller events like dinners with them, taking them to spend the night or see friends, and the many small but wonderful things kids do.

Life lesson: Success in your career comes at a cost to family time.

As I was becoming a father to two boys in 2007, it was these misses that helped me make my decision: I chose being a dad. It was funny. Me becoming a highly successful executive was suddenly in question. I was given special homework to validate our upcoming project plan. It was noted that I would have to go to the "depths of the floors of hell" by my advisors as I planned to be at home for the first Thanksgiving with our boys. My successful career that had led me to the executive level was now in shambles, as I had chosen being a dad over career. That moment really made me realize that if I keep doing what I've been doing, then I'll keep getting what I've been getting, which meant, for me, long hours away from my family on the road and missing out on being a dad. Luckily for me, a senior executive saw the train wreck and helped me out of it by allowing me to work on a special project that led me to building my own department. This new role got me off the road for the next nine years, which allowed me to see my girls make it into their teenage years. So I had been blessed.

As that time passed, and I was moved to a new department for the last five years, I was labeled as "not serious enough" to run a department, so I knew I would need to do my best as I finished up my Toyota career. It was around this time that I realized I had *no regrets* for choosing to be a dad to my two girls and two boys, at a time when both parents need each other to get through the teenage years. That is when I got the card named "Casel's Bible" back from a coworker when I had assembly over ten years before and thought I did make a difference.

I now realize a key fundamental that I learned again from Tony Robbins: "What are you focused on?" What we are focused on decides our feelings and ultimately our reaction. I knew my focus was being a dad, and the reality that I was being pushed aside in my career didn't matter. It still doesn't. In addition to Dad's words, I also hear his voice in Aaron Tippin's song, "You've got to stand for something or you'll fall for anything." Standing up for what's right is not a common choice in large corporations, but it is for a farm boy raised in southern Ohio, Appalachia. As Hank Jr. says, "Country boys can survive," which has been a theme song for me as well.

> **Life lesson: Personal success is more important than corporate success, and it's what really matters, for you need to be able to put your head on the pillow at night with no worries.**

I believe that my constant journey in self-help was a part of my focus to live out my dad's words. My earliest memory of this journey was in high school when I read Robert Schuller's *Tough Times Never Last but Tough People Do*. At the time, I had moved from being a decent trombone player in high school band to just trying to survive two-a-days of high school football. For the first time in my life, I had to dig deep to even step up to the physical endurance of football. While in contrast, my trombone life was one where I seldom practiced outside of school and still seemed to always get the first or second trombone part. I recall not doing well after an early morning football practice and having a temperature of over a hundred degrees Fahrenheit. I went to the coach and explained my struggle. He just told me to get some lunch, hydrate, and rest before the second practice, saying, "You will be fine." I remember doing what coach said and realizing that several others were in the same condition, so I decided to just suck it up. I survived until the end of one very hot two-a-day. I remember getting to the car, cranking up the AC, and suddenly losing over an hour as I had blacked out from the exhaustion of the day. It was through all this that I needed Robert Schuller's lessons of pushing through adversity, and I started to realize the satisfaction and gratification of making it to the other side of adversity, to what felt like victory. As I finished my senior year of high school football, I suddenly felt alive, ready to take on anything. I weighed 165 pounds, benchpressing twice my body weight at 330 pounds. I came out a better, tougher, wiser person who was even more healthy.

I also began to appreciate my family's roots as farmers in Appalachia, as well as for their grit to survive and hard work, which matched the lessons I was learning from Robert Schuller and football. My grandpa Ogle Glenn had told me, "Just remember, as a Burnett, things will never come easy." I felt like it was like a family creed or motto to do and survive the tough times.

As I entered college, I realized how important my lessons on pushing through tough times would be as I started to understand the topics of physics, calculus, and organic chemistry. As I learned that my fellow students had taken those subjects in high school, I felt overwhelmed. During my freshman year of college, I realized it was time for fight or flight. I chose to fight and was so thankful for Robert Schuller, Grandpa Ogle Glenn, football, and my tough, hard-working family. The hours it took to learn those college topics were way more than I had imagined. I recall not only spending long nights studying but also waking up early to get in another round of studying before the class test. I recall getting my first success in organic chemistry, as I understood the fundamentals and was fascinated with applications of plastics that were shared by our professor who was an inventor of plastics medical devices. I studied in a local hotel with a roommate who loved to study, and we actually stayed awake for three and a half days straight to study and take the finals.

I recall that last day in the dorm at Kettering University. I worked my hardest ever at school and left it on the field. I felt that hard work was like breathing, and I could only feel at my best giving it all. Even when I learned my final grade in physics was an F, I was not frustrated or angry, for I had done my best. I knew I had to figure it out and change, for I was determined to be an engineer.

Life lesson: Perseverance and determination are what drives personal success.

As I started my sophomore year in college, I had reenrolled in physics as I transferred to the University of Dayton. About the same time, I learned during my

General Motors co-op from an executive that "luck is the residual of hard work and determination." I had the hard work part down, and soon came the luck. The luck came in the form of an experienced engineering consultant named Dennis Desilets. Dennis was in his fifties and had taken an interest in me because I loved the assembly conveyors running in the plant. He had invented power-and-free conveyors with his mentor, Ade Czarnecki, at a time when he and Ade led the design engineering group at Anchor Conveyors in Detroit, Michigan. Dennis was soon like my own personal engineering professor. He would break my work on conveyor issues down into homework problems. Just like being in school, he would teach a lesson on things like calculating conveyor buffers and pucker factor while also taking me to the shop floor to show me real-world examples of the day's lesson.

My love for engineering flew off the page at the same time that physics came alive for me. At the time, I was just so happy to be learning and understanding how to be an engineer that I never knew how much Dennis had done for me except for the fact that he was sharing his life and how he had learned to have what I now call "no regrets." Dennis grew his passion into a large company called DEC Engineering. He was the *E* in DEC. DEC was no longer in business at the time, for Dennis had made a conscious decision to close it after he met the girl of his life in a Detroit-area cafe. He was in the midst of getting ready to buy out his other two partners when he met this girl. Dennis truly loved just helping people solve their problems, and he realized he had grown his love into a business that consumed his time with accountants worrying over him and with lawyers worrying over liabilities his company had created with designs.

Dennis's girl had suddenly made him aware of the real world, where people just care for each other and help each other, just like what he was now doing for me as an ambitious, young engineer. I will never forget him one early dark morning after a conveyor start-up. We were walking across the rooftop back to the office, and it was a beautiful, starry night with the sunrise just starting to peak up at the horizon. Dennis stopped to rest and enjoy his morning cigarette, leaning against a nearby piece of equipment, saying, "Grasshopper, if I teach you nothing else, remember this. You see all this stuff around us? It's just steel, aluminum, and plastics. It's just stuff without people to turn it into something, so never forget about the people first, for the rest will take care of itself."

Life lesson: Never forget about the people, for the rest is just stuff.

I realize now that moment is one of those lifetime lessons that will be a video or movie that never loses its brilliance. At the time, I felt special, for Dennis had shared something so intimate but never recognized till now how much of an impact Dennis Desilets would have on me. Like my dad's life lessons, Dennis's life lesson had changed my life. As I further reflect on it, I truly believe that moment with Dennis is the reason I happily chose being a dad over a general manager. A general manager would just be responsible for stuff and people to make stuff happen while a dad would be responsible for the precious lives of his children and now even their children. As I have come into the third quarter of my life, halftime in my forties is over. I now know my decision to be a dad was a great one.

I'm now watching those two adopted boys and our girls become young adults. Each one works on their own version of themselves, and they're all doing well, not only in life, but also they're beginning to see the value in people beyond themselves. Two of the four kids now have children of their own, and I love to watch them care and love for their own. I realize the beauty of life as well as I learn while trying to help some of the greatest people I have ever met, which are my grandchildren. Just like the movie *Hope Floats*, I recognize the beauty of being older, to be able to slow down enough to hear those tiny voices, to hear their dreams and answer their questions, while the business of life as a parent makes us unable to always have the time and patience to really know what is on our children's minds. Learning to stop and listen is one of my greatest changes, which again reflects why Dad's words, "If you keep doing what you have been doing, you'll keep getting what you have been getting," are so important. Dad's purpose was to make me realize change was a good thing, for we would never know what's on the other side of it. I believe this is why he chose to leave farming and go to the big city to work in the paper mill with no knowledge of it, just like engineering was for me.

Life lesson: Being open to accepting change is necessary for personal growth.

I had been blessed to also learn from Robert Schuller, football, and Grandpa Ogle Glenn that change required hard work and perseverance to push through it, which my dad had also demonstrated time and again. Those words of his led me to another great change point in my life, which was leaving General Motors and joining to Toyota. This change meant leaving my childhood home and moving to another state, which was Michigan initially. The ironic part of that change was being moved to the automotive capital of the world, which is Detroit, Michigan. As I now had weekends free again with my beautiful wife and a toddler, we found ourselves becoming fans of the Ford

Museum. We enjoyed the summer days of Greenfield Village riding the train, and I loved learning about Henry Ford's love for making things. It was so wonderful to have real-world displays of the assembly line that I could share and explain my life as an engineer in automotive. At the same time, we could share in my love for automobiles with all the vehicles in the Ford Museum and the numerous local car shows and cruise-ins that were held by the many car lovers in the Detroit area. Once again, the willingness to push through the fears of change and learning a new culture in a new company had paid off in my being able to share my life with my family and learning more of my love as an engineer. As I learned about Henry Ford and others like the Dodge Brothers, General Motors founder William Durant, Charles Kettering, and Henry's best friend Thomas Edison, I realized they all had something in common, which was fostering in great changes in the world with hard work and perseverance.

Thomas Edison, in his creation of the light bulb, had over ten thousand failures but knew "sooner or later, the only solution left is the right one." Henry Ford, who had been an employee of Thomas Edison, wanted "to build a car that every man could afford" and found that answer with his development of the assembly line. Charles Kettering never stopped wanting to make or invent things to help make life simpler and safer, like with the creation of the electric starter for the 1912 Cadillac. William "Billy" Durant had the vision to make cars for the masses by buying great car start-ups like Louis Chevrolet Motors, Lasalle, Pontiac, and so on, which allowed people to have options of automobiles that fit their desires, which was then enhanced further with the GM organization leader Alfred Sloan.

At the time, I could not get enough of the amazing automobile history found in Detroit, especially as I continued to visit the Ford Museum and read books on the great names I heard about in the industry. As I visited Japan for the first time and took time to visit the Toyota Industrial and Car Museum, I began to realize my new company's love for automobiles and more importantly, about their focus on engineering. Toyota was not only an auto company that was founded on engineering; it was also led by engineers who first cared about making great things and then worked to make those things profitable. Toyota's love of engineering allowed me to feel right at home and willing to work harder than ever, which truly just felt like what I was supposed to be doing and not like work itself. I was blessed to have great engineers in Toyota Assembly Engineering, like Mr. Hayashi and Mr. Somiya, who believed in what we were doing and never gave up on us as long as were trying. They too lived the words of change with their words, like the new model Sienna being "Mission Impossible," then breaking down the problem alongside me while making it come to life, which made engineering awesome.

As I left Michigan for a new home in Kentucky at Toyota, my resolve to work hard and persevere were tested to the limits while I was in the middle of Mr. Somiya's "Mission Impossible," which was the making of the first-generation Sienna. I ended up being the last man standing from the Detroit-based assembly group, since the others moved on to new companies to stay in the Detroit area, which most of them called their childhood home. This change drove me to learn even more new equipment as I had to take over from those members who left to finish them up with a fellow coworker who, as a part of the variable workforce, was already on the road himself, so the move did not mean anything to him. I found my engineering approach to be evolved as I tried to simplify the physical theories in order to get help from others who were not engineers. For example, the very crucial and complex automation for filling the brake systems was simplified in my explanations as simply a machine that "sucks and blows," which also made the opening conversation lighthearted and thus palatable as we dove into problems with it. For brake fill actually sucked out all the air in the system with a vacuum pump and blew in brake fluid. The issue was finding all the vacuum leaks and/or missing cavities caused by the master cylinder valves.

In retrospect, blowing the brake fluid into the system was a similar issue in reverse. This simplistic approach led us to adjust the valve open/close timing to find these hidden cavities and fix leaks on the brake-fill gun by realizing it was simply the weight of the hoses causing most of the leaks. I now recognize that a simplistic view of a system and breaking it down was exactly what Dennis Desilets taught during those "Grasshopper" engineer years before, so I was lucky to look up and find Dennis who lived in the Detroit area before completely leaving Michigan to thank him for his friendship and teaching. I'm glad now I took the time to thank Dennis, for I just recently learned almost twenty-five years later that he had recently passed away.

Life lesson: Take the time to thank those who have helped us before it is too late to do so.

It is also important that in addition to embracing change to live out the words, "If you keep doing what you have been doing, you'll keep getting what you have been getting," you must also recognize those people who helped you to take the leap of faith and work through the change as well. For even myself, I had chosen engineering because Mr. McCabe, a high-school science teacher who finally became a principal, continually told me, "Don't just work on cars. Become an engineer and build cars."

I recognize how much my parents helped me too, for they never doubted my dreams of going to college and becoming an engineer, even though they had no idea what an engineer did or what physics, which included topics like statics, dynamics, and fluid mechanics, did for us. It is this reason today that I'm fascinated to share knowledge with my grandchildren and hear their ideas on what they want to do and who they want to become. In a similar fashion, it was my general manager who chose to make me a manager while I was on vacation, knowing full well I didn't want the job at the time. That led to another push a few years later to become a senior manager as well.

It's interesting to see how these things have impacted me as an executive and leader, for I found myself acting out my dad's words through others. Recently, I had a senior engineer who chose not to apply for a manager opening in our group. I called her directly and shared the fact there was a manager opening and immediately got her reply, "I don't think I'm interested." I found myself telling her what a manager does and then sharing examples of things she was doing to demonstrate those qualities. In addition, like myself previously, I found her still saying "no" by the words "I'm not sure," so then I just told her, "I'd really like you to apply. I know you can do it." Suddenly, here I was telling someone else to embrace change and just reinforced that she already demonstrated the hard work and perseverance that would be necessary to make it successfully through the change. As an engineer and now as a leader, I even more recognize the power of Dennis's words that starry night years ago, "Grasshopper, if I teach you nothing else, remember this. You see all this stuff around us? It's just steel, aluminum, and plastics. It's just stuff without people to turn it into something, so never forget about the people first, for the rest will take care of itself." At the time, I knew how much Dennis impacted me as an engineer, but now I so recognize his life lesson as a leader who takes care of people and, more importantly, serves people. I now believe this is why servant leadership is becoming a key principle that is being taught to management trainees and leaders.

> **Life lesson: As leaders, we lose our direct single ability to effect change as we take on responsibility in an organization. But the real key is how we can multiply our ability to effect change by how we treat those people working with us.**

Success as a leader starts with embracing change ourselves and then having the ability to lead others to embrace change. In order for change to be successful, we first learn ourselves that change requires hard work and perseverance. With that in mind, you have to follow the people through the change and encourage them by sharing the good and bad points with the reminder that change is a journey and they're going to make it. In addition, on the journey, it's important to truly help them through moments where they are stuck, by breaking down issues into bite-size chunks that they can manage on their own. At the same time, a leader can help by quietly eliminating roadblocks that suddenly make the path ahead appear not only clear but also possible to make it through. As they begin to make it down the path, it's important to help them realize what they did and learned, along with what they said they could not do, so they recognize the power of embracing change and how the hard work and perseverance was worth it and maybe even do it again in the future.

How could I have known my dad's words had such amazing life lessons?

- Be willing to embrace change.
- Realize that hard work and perseverance are necessary ingredients to make change happen.
- Recognize others who helped you to take the path toward change and especially those who helped you with the issues along the way.
- Recognize that people are the reason changes are made and the way to make a difference, so help and encourage others to embrace change.

As I think about it, it further reinforces the journey to *No Regrets* through living out these words from my dad as well as the others. Today, I could imagine what I would have been had I not embraced their words:

- An auto mechanic in my childhood home fixing one person's car at a time versus an engineering executive who helps the company make a new car that is provided to a new person every minute from over a dozen different plants in North America
- A General Motors engineer who became a supervisor in a single location versus an engineering executive managing engineering at eighty-two sites that not only produce cars but also sell cars, deliver cars to dealers, and provide the parts to fix them

As noted, these changes did not come easy, for there were people who tried stopping me. Some were angry at me and just added to the noise while I was trying to stay focused on hard work and perseverance. During these times of extreme noise, you have to stay the course and believe in the process of hard work and determination.

As you become accustomed to the process, you will begin to recognize and appreciate those lucky moments when it appears that divine intervention has stepped in, and it most likely has. For the words I learned, "Luck is the residual of hard work and determination," also closely matches the words I learned from Robert Schuller: "Work as if it depends on you and pray as if it depends on him." I believe those prayers must include thanks to the higher power and also thanks to him for bringing those people around who helped you through issues found as your worked through the change.

I believe that even the higher power expects us to change, for he wants to provide us help in the process and make it to the other side that feels like a victory, even if it's only for ourselves. I also believe it needs Dad's words of faith in yourself: "You can do anything if you put your mind to it." Hard work and perseverance need moments of focus and reflection to not only solve issues but also embrace further adjustments along the way to make it through adversity.

As a person who has made changes for myself, I never would have realized the multiplying effect of doing so, because I became an engineer before I became an engineering executive that was able to help hundreds of engineers. In turn, the engineers were able to help thousands of production team members build millions of cars for new customers, so they could care for themselves, their families, and their friends. Customers used those cars to move people and help them care for themselves, their families, and friends by moving people and things. In return, they can make changes for people so they, in turn, can change things themselves. What an amazing butterfly effect caused by one person willing to make a change themselves!

As I think about the size of the impact from these thoughts and words that were turned into action, it truly makes me recognize more and more why I wanted to take the time to share my dad's help and life lessons. Through the actions I've taken from his words, I am honored to learn and say I have no regrets about the changes I've made in my life.

As I further reflect, I want change and the willingness to make it to continue for the remainder of my life. I helped and watched my own family make change and see how much better off they are for it. I recently helped my parents move out of my childhood home that my dad had finished building and into a new space where they have help with cooking and cleaning while still keeping their independence.

I am watching and helping them with the struggle of change leaving a familiar place brings, but now I see them enjoying new friends and new events with those new acquaintances. At the same time, I am seeing their old friends move on, and I am so happy they can fill those holes with new people and things. Even for myself, we have chosen to move out of our family home of over sixteen years into a condo in a senior-based community. With less space to maintain, I now have the time and space to be finally writing this book, which further reinforces my life of *No Regrets*.

Even though the move from a large house on six acres to a condo required us to simplify and reduce, we now realize how many things we had forgotten we had and now can enjoy. The smaller space takes less time to maintain the things we enjoy, and thus, it even becomes more joyful as we get to feel and see the value in it. Without helping my parents and seeing the struggle and benefit of simplifying, I could have seen us staying in our home.

At the same time, I realize we were struggling to maintain that large space as well. Similar to what I found with my parents, pieces of our home were not only incomplete but also in a state of disrepair. In addition, it was gratifying to hear the new owners be so excited to get our home, which further justified the change and the benefits of Dad's words, "If you keep doing what you have been doing, you'll keep getting what you have been getting." Ironically, he said those words to me on the porch of that large home on the six acres as I considered purchasing it sixteen years earlier, so change was good then, as it is going to be good again. Thanks, Dad, again for your words and life lessons.

NEVER STOP LEARNING

I remember hearing those words from my dad as I headed off to college. At the time I was the first one in our family to go to college, so it made sense. I remember talking to him one evening about my internal combustion engines class. Out of the blue, he asked, "Do you know how fuel injection works?" So I shared that it basically uses the fuel pump to spray fuel into the air stream at just the right time for the combustion process. The next thing I know, he was sketching a carburetor on a notepad and comparing what I told him to an air-aspirated carburetor and said, "Hmm, it works the same. They just eliminated the jets and made it simpler. That makes sense." I stood there mesmerized as I realized how my dad used his previous detailed knowledge to understand a new technology by making a sketch to comprehend it so fast.

Life lesson: It is important to understand the past to be better able to understand the future.

In addition to learning about the future, you have to be curious and willing to accept change as well. I found myself from that moment on looking more closely at the history of automobiles to see how things have evolved. As

I compared brakes from the Ford Model T, which were completely manual, to the 1970s General Motors brake system, which didn't only have a master hydraulic cylinder but also added disc brakes, I saw how physics and the use of hydraulics created the ability to apply more brake force, thus allowing a greater stopping power.

As I compared the wheels of the Ford Model T to the split rims of the 1930s automobiles, to the solid steel rims of current vehicles, I could see how wheels from the carriage days, which were solid wood, had evolved to wood spokes that attached to an inflated tire on a steel rim, and ultimately, that led to the solid steel-rim tires of today, which allows for safer wheel assembly, thus simplifying repairs.

As I compared steering systems of the Ford Model T to today's systems, I can see how things evolved from a manual gear-driven system to a hydraulic pump-assisted power steering system, and finally to today's steer-by-wire systems, which reduce the power needs of the engine and simplify vehicle structure. As I did this, I began to realize how change had improved vehicle safety by simpler repairs, reliability through simpler designs, and improved efficiency by simpler structures.

It was also in this moment when Dad showed his practice of understanding the past that I started to grasp and understand those common-sense practices. For example, my dad's cheater bar approach to breaking bolts loose on cars made so much sense when I understood torque equals force times distance. Similarly, when splitting wood, keeping your hands at the bottom of the handle and swinging directly overhead also demonstrated physics, with torque equaling force times distance, or more commonly known as a moment arm.

From those lessons, I started to realize my own personal observations, like, "Why does smoke go up a chimney?" which took a few physics theories to explain: High pressure seeks lower pressure caused by the heat going up the chimney. Or air blowing over the top of the chimney causes a lower pressure above the chimney while no velocity inside the chimney causes high pressure, thus forcing the smoke out of the chimney.

This all happened just prior to meeting Dennis Desilets, who then showed me how to be an engineer inside of an assembly plant. The common-sense approach from Dennis matched as well and showed me how things like a seat flipper on a conveyor was simply a moment arm. Once again, physics and torque equals force times distance came to the rescue. He helped me convert the pounds of force using an air cylinder into PSI (pounds per square inch) so that I could more accurately set up the seat flipper equipment.

This new understanding led me to my successful understanding of statics as now a moment arm was the basis of the summation of moments around a pivot point to determine the forces and the ultimate required load on members. From there, my interest expanded to kinematics of machines, where moments also determine things like angular velocity and, thus, the necessary size and ratios of the gears.

Suddenly, my life as an engineer was helping me to understand the theory behind the many common-sense things my dad had taught me while working. It was fascinating for me to move from trial-and-error approaches to a more satisfactory result by being able to use equations from physics as well as get to the result quicker. I realized as I better understood things through my dad's "Never stop learning" that my thirst for learning grew, which then led to so-called perpetual learning.

This new recognition that understanding history, just like the equations from theories, would allow me to better understand or imagine the future not only expanded my desire to study and compare vehicle designs but also led me to an interest in American history. As I began to wonder about the origin of the USA and its democracy, I began to read about the struggle that led to the American Revolution of 1776. As I understood the importance of the Founding Fathers, I began to study and read about each of them to understand more about them.

I also found common threads. Each founding father was a successful businessman, or what is known today as an entrepreneur. Due to their desire to make a perfect union, it was fascinating to learn how they themselves studied the history of various governments. From their desire to never stop learning, they combined the good pieces of several historical governments to create a more balanced organization so that its processes drove checks and balances. This was to avoid the problems of a monarchy, like the ones found in Rome. US founders did not want a single government executive that could encourage tyranny.

As I continued learning American history, I combined my book learning from things like "The Frontiersman" with travel to key historic places and really became fascinated by the American spirit and the journey to the West. As I looked more closely at St. Louis, Missouri, the "Gateway to the West," I realized it had references back to Cincinnati, Ohio, as I followed the Budweiser family history. I looked more closely at Cincinnati, Ohio, and the Cincy Museum Center, where I saw references to Harpers Ferry, West Virginia, as the previous gateway to the West. As I visited all three of these historical places, I saw one clear thing in common: the River. In addition to the River, you did feel like you came through a passage or gateway as you looked back to the East from where you had come. It was exciting to be there, and I could imagine heading West with your family and everything you own, which couldn't be much considering you're either on foot, horseback, or at best, a covered wagon.

My "Never stop learning" journey of American history started with my daughter's school trip to Washington DC, where I was reminded of our country's great Founding Fathers, like George Washington, Thomas Jefferson, Ben Franklin, and John Adams, to name a few. During the school trip, we were blessed to visit the home of George Washington, where I realized how he had a family farm that was a business, so he was an entrepreneur. George was not only a successful landowner, following up on what he learned as a surveyor; he was also an experimenter with agricultural approaches. He also shared his struggle of using tobacco as a cash crop. George not only had a private secretary, but he also had a farm manager and a distillery manager for his whiskey distillery. George even had a Potomac River Fishery in his closing years. George's Mount Vernon made me realize our Founding Fathers were already successful businessmen, and their fight for freedom was not because they were poor or a slave to the British monarchy. For the Founding Fathers, the freedom from Britain was about each and every person being able to be their own unique individual self and to live out the dream of their choosing.

At Thomas Jefferson's Monticello, my learning journey made me realize how Thomas was like a scientist. As a part of the Lewis and Clark Expedition, which he legislated funding for, Thomas was fascinated to learn of what we now know were wooly mammoth fossils from the modern-day Big Bone Lick State Park in Kentucky. I even visited Big Bone Lick State Park to learn of the salt licks left from the Ice Age, which is why the wooly mammoths came there and were often trapped by the bogs that were part of the salt lick. I imagined Lewis and Clark being stunned at finding the large bones of a wooly mammoth in the wilderness and wondering, "Are any of them still alive and right around where I'm standing here?"

Back at Monticello, I realized Thomas was also an entrepreneur as his family farm was a business. Thomas even wrote to George Washington while he was in Paris as a foreign diplomat, "Agriculture…is our wisest pursuit, because it will in the end contribute most to wealth, good morals, and happiness." Thomas, like George, experimented with plant species, production techniques, and soil. Thomas not only produced crops but also raised cattle for beef, milk, and butter, using manure as fertilizer. At the same time, Thomas was inspired by the natural wonders of Virginia that are found along the Shenandoah Valley. Thomas's Monticello made me realize once again how our Founding Fathers were successful businessmen and entrepreneurs and how their fight for freedom was not about being poor or a slave to Britain. For the Founding Fathers, it was about being free as an individual to enjoy the beauties and natural wonders of such a great world and country we live in.

In my study of Benjamin Franklin at Philadelphia, my learning desires also led me to recognize how Mr. Franklin was also an entrepreneur. Franklin not only had a printing press in Philadelphia where he wrote *Poor Richard's Almanack*, but he also leased them up and down the East Coast in an effort to let people know what's going on and communicate with them, which was a precursor to today's Facebook. Franklin also invented famous things like bifocals, the lightning rod, and a musical instrument called the glass armonica. Franklin used his idea of the Junto and his printing presses to proliferate and get support for causes that led Philadelphia to having the first public library, the first volunteer fire company, and the nation's first hospital. Franklin had come from Boston to Philadelphia in search of work at the Quaker City, where its people were given privileges and religious freedom under the charter of William Penn. Franklin knew that liberty and tolerance were the keys to a civil society.

Franklin's Philadelphia made me realize again how the founders were successful businessmen and entrepreneurs, and their fight for freedom was not because they were poor or a slave to a monarchy. For the Founding Fathers, it was about the pursuit of happiness that comes from the ideals of liberty and tolerance. It was these ideals that led these great men and Founding Fathers to study and create a government where a well-balanced system of democracy ensured their people a lifetime of liberty and ensured the necessary mechanisms from law and order to ensure tolerance of the people. I walked away from Philadelphia proud of our country and amazed at the commitment, heart, and soul of our Founding Fathers. I was amazed at the sacrifice and courage of our Founding Fathers, who had nothing to gain and everything to lose as they chose to not only support but engage in the fight for freedom.

The Founding Fathers made the conscious decision to go up against the largest monarchy in the world, Great Britain, while not knowing if the people of the future USA would be able to fight back due to not only a lack of commitment and perseverance but also to a lack of military resources. At that moment, my desire to never stop learning took on a whole new level. I began to appreciate not only the life lessons but also learned that my dad's values of hard work and determination came from a family who were Quakers from Chester County, a suburb of Philadelphia. Thanks, Dad, again for this wonderful life lesson!

On our way back from Philadelphia, we stopped at Valley Forge, Pennsylvania, where George Washington and his troops had stopped during winter. It was hard to imagine being a soldier marching barefoot in the snow. The troops, due to the lack of facilities and cleanliness, had outbreaks of typhoid and dysentery. Out of about twelve thousand troops, two thousand were lost during the six months they had been there during the winter.

This experience of "Never stop learning" really made me appreciate that freedom isn't free. Since the American Revolution, brave soldiers like the ones at Valley Forge have made huge sacrifices in order for us to gain and maintain our freedom. I recognize that my needing to help others through my home and work life is nothing compared to the sacrifices our American soldiers are making each and every day. Long hours and travel are nothing compared to walking into life-threatening situations, not only for yourself, but also for your fellow soldiers. I am forever grateful for Valley Forge teaching me the sacrifices that are made daily for our freedom.

In another trip to learning about American history, I took our family to Boston, Massachusetts. It was fascinating to see the porch where the Declaration of Independence was declared from, especially after being delivered from Philadelphia. I could not imagine the pressure on the person riding horseback carrying such an important document as requested. The pressure on the reader of the Declaration of Independence had to be immense as well, for in this trip, I realized the presence of the British. The British soldiers were roaming the streets in an attempt to keep law and order. The British soldiers were also intimidating; they carried guns and wore well-appointed suits. Realizing also that Boston was a harbor to the ocean made the threat of the British soldiers real, for their mode of travel and movement was the water, and they could move easily between the harbor and the ocean. The word of the Declaration was spread through handbills and could easily be captured by the British soldiers. Imagine being caught holding them or distributing them! I could imagine being captured and the extreme interrogation the British may have done out of fear of losing control, which is surely why those first few shots were fired during an uprising in Boston against people who were not even armed themselves.

I sat in the church near Paul Revere's home, imagining myself trying to honor the higher power, and off in the distance hearing sounds from the clashes between Great Britain and the revolutionary soldiers. I realized the US was not even a country yet with common rules and ideals, so what a challenge it was then to even start a war with soldiers in this situation! It made me consider the struggle of communicating the ideals of the Declaration of Independence due to travel being done by horseback, the reality that the British soldiers were well organized and trained, and the realization that they could easily stop and control things as they saw fit. I believe this confidence of being able to easily control things is what led them to put down their guard. At the same time, the New Americans learned guerilla-type warfare from the Native Americans while trying to settle in the wilderness in their new homes. The revolutionary soldiers were able to conduct surprise attacks on the British while using the American wilderness as a shield. It was funny to learn that the British could not use their typical training of warfare. They kept showing up in an organized line of attack in an open field, only to find themselves being shot at from the woods by the revolutionary soldiers. For the New Americans, the only issue was the lack of resources, like guns, ammunition, and food. It took the Founding Fathers of the future USA to realize this and to find funding and resources from the country of France.

As I have continued learning, I realized France's motivation to help the revolution. The French knew Great Britain's world dominance, so they bet on a group of revolutionists in hopes they could begin to break down Great

Britain's dominance. I wonder how the Founding Fathers shared their strategy as well. I could imagine Franklin and Jefferson crafting the story of how Washington's troops could win the war with their "surprise" attacks and how the snobbish, well-organized British armies would stick to their approach even when it was obvious they were beginning to lose battles. I could imagine the French listening to the Founding Fathers share the vastness of the New America and that there was plenty of land for them to get things like furs from the animals to feed their clothing industry. I can imagine the French thinking the New Americans' country would be ripe for the future picking of a more established and sophisticated country like France, and what a deal it was! Just by providing money and resources, they may set up the perfect situation for a future takeover!

My fascination with American history led me on a journey to learn more about the Burnett ancestry in the United States. Thanks to the federal census, I was able to find my third great-grandfather, Peter Burnett, who was previously believed to be a great uncle. As I continued my study of the Burnetts, who were believed to be from Delaware, I found we were actually from Chester County, Pennsylvania. We migrated to Ohio from Pennsylvania via the commonly used trails and the rivers, which reminded me of the Go West movement and the establishment of the "Gateway to the West" cities like Harpers Ferry, Cincinnati, and St. Louis.

I realize how my thirst for learning allows me to cross-pollinate new understandings to better clarify the past as I continue to understand. I realize a key in learning is to realize that the truth is only what you perceive you know from reality. Based on a person's exposure, what appears to be a person making a bad choice could really be just a lack of experience. I now realize that's why some people's truth looks to be a lie, but it's actually due to the lack of experience and understanding. This lack of experience and understanding is genuinely impacted by knowledge, which is gained by experience, which then leads people to genuinely trust or not base on what they observe of that person in a real-world situation. Thanks, Dad, for teaching me to never stop learning.

During my thirty-two trips to Japan, I had several chances to study the the country's history. My earliest trips took me first to the Toyota History Museum. I soon realized how the Toyoda Company was founded on the looms for the textile industry. In fact, the founder, Sakichi Toyoda, was the one who patented the G loom's ability to detect the broken thread. This invention revolutionized the weaving process. It ensured a quality textile by allowing a broken thread to be fixed prior to impacting the product. This invention today is used in the TPS (Toyota Production System) training to explain *poka-yoke* or double-check devices. I further realized that the loom funded the development of the automobile by letting his son Kiichiro develop the first car as a modern-day Skunk Works project in the back corner of the loom factory. I realized how progressive the thinkers were in the Toyoda family and imagined Toyoda workers who saw what was going on thinking, *What? Are they doing developing a car? There are not even roads in Japan to put a car on.* It was clear that the Toyoda companies were founded and run by engineers, for Toyoda is all about solving problems. It is this ideal of "solving problems to help people" that inspired Sakichi, as he saw his own family's struggles with using looms to make a living.

For myself, it is the reason that I made a career out of working at Toyota Motors Manufacturing, for those same ideals are in our company today. I realize my passion for organizing and fixing things are about solving problems, and that's why I have enjoyed my Toyota life even with some long days and struggles. In those early trips to the history museum, I learned why the Japanese culture was so conservative. They lived on an island with limited resources. They had to conserve using the bare minimum materials and had to reuse things. This conservative approach also meshed well with my upbringing by Appalachian farmers who were also limited in resources due to being a part of a poorer community with little access to education. It was the lack of access to resources that forced farmers to reuse and fix materials that built in problem solving as well. In addition, Japan's culture was based on agriculture due to rice crops, which meshed well with my family of farmers that raised tobacco.

As my trips to Japan continued, my next adventures led me to the Toyoda Automobile Museum. My first "Never stop learning" moment was recognizing how the first automobile, the 1937 AA Toyoda Sedan, was created. The AA Sedan was a mixture of the Chrysler Airflow for its sleek look and fuel efficiency and the Chevrolet Sedan for its stable driving caused by the design of putting the engine over the center line of the front axle. It suddenly made me realize why, even today, we study competitor's vehicles, taking the best parts of each vehicle to make an even better automobile. It was fascinating to learn the original processes of manufacturing car parts, like the fender where curves were hand-rolled with the dies and adjusted like a blacksmith does with horseshoes. These experiences led me to further study the automobile back home in Michigan. I expanded my understanding of automobile design by studying Harley Earl, who made the amazing General Motors designs for the 1950s Corvette and the tail fins of the Cadillac, as the USA was fascinated with the space race at the time. Earl's designs also capitalized on the General Motors architecture created by Alfred Sloan, who wanted customers for life by creating a lineup of car companies that customers could grow into.

Sloan's strategy was to design entry-level cars like Chevrolet that were also efficient, and Pontiac where you could get some raw power. Sloan then added Buick and Oldsmobile next in the lineup as that entry-level customer wanted more, so Buick had great ride comfort while Oldsmobile had that plus rawer but sophisticated power. Sloan then made Cadillac as the luxury vehicle, where the most sophisticated buyers could get the ultimate ride, accessories, and power. Cadillac also gave General Motors a place to try and refine new technology while recouping the costs in the naturally higher price. The kid who just wanted to be an auto mechanic was really beginning to learn the making of an automobile, and it was fascinating, all thanks to my dad's teachings. I visited Japan learning about Toyota and then came back home to compare those lessons learned to the American automobile industry.

My initial love for working on cars now had become a passion, and it led me on a journey to study the history of the automobile in the USA. The Toyota Automobile Museum taught me how Kiichiro had come to the US in the 1930s to study Ford, who had recently developed the assembly line. Like Kiichiro, I began to understand the great impact and advantage of the assembly line, as I was able to see it live in displays at the Ford Museum. The Ford Museum had working models of the conveyor, and I could now see the vision of Henry Ford, which was bringing the parts to the assembly worker to minimize the time required. The assembly line also drove Henry to standardize design of parts and their manufacturing so they would go together in the same way and not require rework or unique craftsman to build a vehicle, like the horseless carriage the new automobile design replaced.

I was fascinated as I was an assembly production engineer at the time at Toyota, and this new understanding of assembly lines allowed me to be a better designer of assembly processes. Once again, my dad's "Never stop learning" was really allowing me to become a better engineer while also enjoying learning about history which is another passion of mine.

Life lesson: As we continue to never stop learning, relationships between things starts to develop.

I was intrigued even more as I realized that Henry Ford's drive to "Make a car that any man could afford" had created a new problem, as people needed a place to drive their newly purchased automobile. The new automobile or horseless carriage was being used on roads that also were still being used by horses with wagons and carriages that left deep ruts after some severe weather. The automobile had an engine that could reach much higher speeds, for those engines had the ability to create multiple horsepower. The automobile driver needed a better place to drive their car, so I soon began to study the history of our highway system.

The first dream of a coast-to-coast road was a project that came to be called the "Lincoln Highway." First conceptualized by Carl Fisher, who had successfully created the Indianapolis 500, Fisher thought he could privately fund the project with a minimal charge to automobile makers and their accessory makers. In 1912, there were over 2.5 million miles of roads that were dirt from the days of horse and carriages. Fisher finally got the commitment of two men from the automobile industry, Frank Sieberling, the president of Goodyear Tire, and Henry Joy, the president of Packard Motor Car Corporation. In order to gain further support, Henry Joy developed the idea of seeding miles, which was a one-mile stretch of concrete every fifty miles. The thinking was the public would see the benefits of concrete and would begin demanding it from their local governments. The idea of "Coming Soon—the Lincoln Highway" made a lot of sense as I imagined more new car drivers were increasing every day due to the Ford cars. Henry Ford would not support the Lincoln Highway project. He believed the public government should provide the funding and not the private industry; otherwise, maintenance of the roads would not be sustained by the local government. I can see both arguments. The private sector would help increase the desire for new cars with roads, and the public sector would ensure new ownership and maintenance of the roads with taxes from the road economy. By 1921, the federal government passed the Federal Highway Act of 1921, which allowed for $75 million of matching funds to the states for highway construction. Eventually, this led to the numbered highway system that we know today. For an auto mechanic turned engineer, it was fascinating to see how Ford's idea of "Making a car that any man can afford" led to the development of the auto industry and the necessary things to support it, such as parts makers, highway systems, and ultimately, small businesses along the highway.

Life lesson: Development of one industry ultimately creates opportunities for other new industries.

As I have driven parts of the Lincoln Highway and Route 66, it is apparent how the automobile drove the idea of fast food, drive-ins, drive-thru, souvenirs, shopping, and services to people who are on the road, as well as the creation of motel and hotel chains like the Holiday Inn. My passion to work on cars was fueled by my "Never stop learning" spirit as I continued to learn about the automobile industry and its impact on society. As people could move to greater distances in a shorter time, the idea of vacations further enhanced things like food and places to stay along the road as it developed. People now could live in the suburbs and commute to the city for work, which eliminated the need for as much housing in the city and led to cities now having expansive areas made up of suburbs. People were now able to enjoy the less hectic suburbs and still get the benefits of a city with a quicker commute.

My learning experience with the automobile industry made me realize the benefit and impact of a particular good like the automobile and the potential extended services like fast foods, motels, hotels, etc., that can be offered to enhance the experience. As I consider that in today's world, the ability to Google locations of a local restaurant allows one to further expand the impact of service and convenience.

Even for myself, the automobile has given me the time and freedom to venture out during business trips. One example is Balboa Park in San Diego, California. This 1,200-acre community park is not just home to green space for rest and relaxation but also has museums, walking paths, theaters, gift shops, restaurants, and even the San Diego Zoo. This space allows me to learn about the area's history and experience things with the local people.

As I have experienced cultures and people, I have made some intentional choices to put myself in new situations with people I'm not familiar with. One such learning choice was to become part of the industry board for Woodward High School in Cincinnati, Ohio. As part of the group to enhance the experience at Woodward by making sure it considered how to educate kids for industry, I chose to spend a few weeks teaching a class on "Being an Engineer" in manufacturing. My focus was to share the kinds of things an engineer does to solve problems. After sharing various types of areas that engineers can work in, I spent some time showing the students the role of an engineer and how writing an equipment specification helps answer the questions of the 5Ws and 1H—who, what, when, where, why, and how. Not knowing whether I was making a difference, I was surprised to be approached by one of the quieter students who thanked me and noted, "Mr. Burnett, I've been thinking, and I think I can become an engineer." At that moment, I knew I made a difference and shared that anyone can learn if they put their mind to it. During that experience, I learned so much about the life of an inner-city student. For them, life at school was about survival, so school was a safe, comfortable place to be for a few hours and have a decent meal. School was also about an escape from the worry of being harassed, beaten up, or even shot at. School for them was a place where people cared about them. During a review of capstone projects, I realized only one parent showed up out of twenty students. I realized at that moment how lucky I was to have parents who cared and a dad who was teaching me life lessons.

I realized learning was not just about me and my skills; it is also about learning to care for others. Even if that caring is just about taking the time to listen, answer questions, or just simply be there to learn about them. It reminds me of Grandma Lestie, who taught me about the "school of life." She grew up going to some single-room schools, never went to college, but her common-sense approach to life and people was off the charts. Grandma Lestie had a special way and a sense to encourage people to go and learn, just like she did for me going to college.

Life lesson: I realize that "Never stop learning" is about connecting our experiences in order to understand new things, like my dad did when he compared the fuel injection today to the air-aspirated ones of the past.

By connecting things and learning more about them, a person can make better sense of the ways things are and why they are that way. Thanks, Dad, for another life lesson.

GET AT IT

I was intentional with putting this chapter last, for it's key to making all the other life lessons from my dad work. "Get at it" is all about "taking action." I smile even when I say it because it brings back those wonderful memories of working with my dad. He and I were at our best when we were putting our hands to work. My dad never hesitated to just get at it. At the time, I just figured he was trying to get it done and accepted it as the way it was.

As I have gotten older and began to organize my thoughts for this book, I realize the amazing power of getting at it. Getting at it is the difference between thinking about it and making something happen. From my engineering world, I would call it "analysis paralysis." As an individual, I realized for some reason that I always was getting things done, and I would see others struggling. I first noticed this as an engineer at General Motors, working job requests for items needed for production on the shop floor. Whether it was a new hoist, drinking fountain, or an ergonomic assist, I would find myself jumping in to create a design and, when stuck, quickly asking questions to our local vendors and to the maintenance team to find answers and move on.

Life lesson: I now realize "not being afraid to ask questions and ask for help" was a key to successfully starting and finishing things.

At the same time, I would organize all the materials for those jobs to make sure everything was ready. I would meet with the responsible maintenance team members before the job started to review the drawings and material cut sheets to discuss any settings or adjustments to be made to various pieces such as pressure valves. I now realize that communication and collaboration allowed me to learn from the experience of the maintenance team members and gain their commitment to getting the work done.

As I moved on to larger projects at General Motors, I realized others' hesitation, as I had to rely on their support to be successful. I would see it in the output of trades people who almost seemed to be stopped at the work they were performing. I would soon learn they needed a tool to perform a task or needed some knowledge that would allow them to get at it. As I later studied Walt Disney and his success at WED (Walter Elias Disney) Enterprises, Walt's analogy to being like a bee pollinating flowers was his way of describing the importance of following up with his team. This follow-up requires a trust with your team to allow you into their world. Depending on the situation, the follow-up can start with just a simple conversation of "How are you doing?" If there are pending issues, such as major delays, then a follow-up may need to start with the words, "Where are we struggling?" The key to making people trust and let you in is making sure you are in this with them, and they are not on an island. Another key to further progress is being willing to work with them on the issue at hand, whether being a resource yourself or providing access to a resource that can help.

As I began to do major shutdowns and reconfigurations of entire conveyor systems at General Motors, I realized another important point, which was motivating others. I saw this as we were preparing for a new future paint shop, which required a 24/7 approach to successfully perform thirty-two tie-in points and a start-up in about nine days, which included some major demolition and rework. We had a team of experienced conveyor engineers but realized the "wow" in their faces in the last couple of weeks of meeting and preparing for the shutdown.

In reflection about that time, I realize now that they were lacking confidence in our ability to get everything done on time. To help them gain confidence, I realized people were not clear on their assignments and how to communicate completion, since the thirty-two areas were spread across more than a million square feet and two floors. I decided to create a "combat room," or central place, to post and maintain our progress from each shift so we could then confirm readiness for start-up. In those detailed discussions of the plan in the last week, the team even helped me realize ways we could "trial" pieces of the system while completing other areas. As I organized a visual board to track tie-in completions, the team was assigned areas to support the individual "trials," and suddenly, I could feel the confidence coming in. It was all happening around the time of my first daughter's birth at nearby Kettering Hospital.

In the midst of becoming a father, I will never forget stopping by a portrait of the hospital founder Charles Kettering, which had a simple quote of his words: "Nothing ever built | Arose to touch the skies | Unless one man willed that it should | Unless one man willed that it must." At that very moment, full of emotion for soon becoming a father and the excitement of a major shutdown, I remember saying to myself, "I am that one man." I remember the last review of our plans in the combat room and stating those daring words of Charles F. Kettering. I reminded the team of the importance of these changes so we could move forward with a new paint shop and a new model Blazer that would help secure the future for the people of this plant. I had this team come together for a huddle like before a big football game, and we made a rally cry. We did have a successful shutdown and start-up, but it took late nights and studying our conditions in the combat room where we pulled ahead and adjusted trials to be able to make it in the end.

> **Life lesson: As I reflect on all of this, I realize getting at it takes confidence—confidence in yourself and others to do their part.**

That confidence comes from a clear plan in your mind, which may require breaking things down on paper. Ironically, I did exactly that as I prepared to write *No Regrets*. I made a digital to-do list of the ten chapters with a due date based on one chapter per week. I further broke each week into five daily sprints of writing that allowed me to track my progress. This gave me the confidence to get at it. Thanks, Dad!

As I moved on to Toyota, those efforts of organizing things and breaking down the work led me to doing more of the same as an individual engineer at Toyota. To make my visits to the Georgetown plant of over 1.5 million square feet efficient, as I had projects in multiple shops of the plant, I utilized a layout of the plant to create a visual plan, or *Kamishibai*, as we call it at Toyota, to determine the most efficient route for my process investigations. The Kamishibai let me consider the shortest distance as well as estimate my investigation time, which required me to make a clear list of items needed. As the list became clear, I then added details of tools required, like a tape measure, and the people to ask info from, like the maintenance or production team, ideally, with a member name. It was interesting to see the plant team members ask me about what I was doing and show sincere surprise at seeing how I had organized my checklist with what, who, and where. That surprise ultimately led to confidence in what I was doing and inspired them to want to help me more.

As an engineer, my "Get at It" mindset led me to being done first with not only the installation but also with the trials of the new spare tire robot the following winter shutdown. On the way out the door for New Year's Day, I was asked if I could help with projects that were behind. I had never worked on that equipment before, but I knew confidence, communication, and collaboration would allow me to get at it to solve the issues with the equipment delays.

On the first piece of equipment, I learned from the maintenance folks that they didn't know the fill volume, so I found that out from a coworker, then realized I needed to add an adjustment to the sensor, and finally, I was able to get it running.

The second equipment was a little more complicated, for the design of the fill tool would not let us set the right level at the end of the cycle, so we added a temporary tool to do so at the end of the cycle. All this quick work was done by communication and collaboration with the maintenance team and the machine maker instilled with the mindset from myself explaining who, what, and why we needed to get at it.

> **Life lesson:** As a manager in engineering, I realized that I had learned an important life lesson as a production supervisor at General Motors: to get at it with a team, someone has to make a decision, even if it's wrong at first.

By setting a direction, which ideally should have a why, the team starts moving things forward, and if decision starts to appear wrong, you can quickly adjust to make it right. As I learned from Stephen Covey, the beauty of human beings is that we have the ability to make wrong decisions right by using our mind and making a change. The key is to make a decision and get at it. I realize now that that's what my dad did with his projects as I watched him adjust a wall dimension to miss an interference or move a sink vanity over if it interfered with opening the door or drawers. My dad's sketch was close enough to get started. He knew that he could not get at it unless he just started and then modified as needed to make it right.

I have seen many projects fail due to engineers being afraid to make a decision, even in a culture of continuous improvement, or *kaizen*, which allows you the perfect reason to change and make it right. To make a decision requires us to make an assumption, or more correctly, an educated guess, but by doing so, you can then use communication and collaboration to confirm with the potential users if it's "close enough," as my dad would say. If the assumption is completely wrong, then my experience is that users may not know what they do want, but for sure, they will tell you what they don't want, which gets you one step closer. This general approach has helped me and my teams multiple times to get off dead center and move forward.

As a manager during a major project, while we were doubling the length of a line, no one could imagine us being able to do this over a winter shutdown. The key assumption they missed was we can install everything but the tie-ins, like I had years before for General Motors. By using weekends prior to the winter shutdown to install pieces right up to the tie-in point, we minimized the time required for the installation. Similar to the GM experience, I visualized the various tie-in points, assigned ownership, made a war room to meet and track progress, which included ways to trial parts of the system as soon as we could. In the end, we doubled the length of the lines. My mistake was not detailing out and designating an owner for the electrical changes like I did for the mechanical ones. Due to lack of focus on electrical tie-ins, we ran successfully for forty-five minutes, and suddenly, the line went down due to lost I/O (inputs/outputs) on the PLC (programmable logic controller). We found the I/O cards, which were 24 VDC, were burnt, the root cause being a forgotten 120 VAC wire being left in the wire tray feeding the burnt cards.

As a testimony to making a decision to get at it, my team noted that the Andon boards, which let us know if we were okay or not for production, along with the motor starters, which give the power to make the conveyors run, and the e-stop system, which shut down the system in the event of an emergency, still worked even though the brain or I/O was not working. I assigned several of my team to be at each panel to activate motor starters for each drive, at each drive motor to be ready to e-stop if anyone yelled a concern over the radio, and a person at the Andon panel to tell the group to go (activate the motor starter) or stop (deactivate the motor starter). We ran the line like that for one and a half hours while our machine maker procured new I/O cards and determined if 120 VAC was to be installed somewhere or demolished. We made the fix at break and lunchtime, which let the plant meet their production numbers for the day so together we got at it.

As were adding a new line in a new facility, we found ourselves with a new plant, all new conveyors, and no new equipment, for it was behind schedule. The equipment was coming from Japan, and they were delayed from having to design first-time equipment that could run both a frame and unibody (H-frame) vehicle on the same line. It was still empty, with only six weeks before going live with vehicle build trials, which was based on equipment arrival dates. Once again, we had to get at it by breaking down the work. Historically, we received two to three trucks per day of overseas containers, but we were going to receive thirteen to fifteen trucks per day this time. In addition, we needed to quickly tear down the containers and keep them in an organized fashion.

We built an assembly line for receiving a sea container, with a leader who would be at a common receiving area, then confirm inside the plant where it went and would tell the forklift driver which parking spot it went to for later pickup and installation. As our contractors confirmed the need for a crate, that same leader would call the forklift driver to pick up crates at a specific spot and have them delivered to the teardown area, where a specialized crew would safely tear down the crates. Finally, once equipment identification was confirmed, the same leader would phone the installers to come pick up the equipment. This process allowed us to cut our prep time, and we were able to successfully install all the equipment before the six weeks were up.

By assigning line leaders who studied equipment drawings and assembly, they could quickly assist contractors in the installation so no time was wasted in figuring out the assembly. Once again, prior to kicking off all the activity, I had to re-instill confidence in the team by reminding them of our teardown strategy, with the assistance with the line leaders. We knew what to do, and we knew we could make it, but we had to stay focused, help each other track progress in the war room, and get at it. And, we did.

As I moved from assembly to powertrain, I began to study their approach to change over and felt the "Get at

It" from assembly had got up and left in powertrain. They had no issue with building ahead to allow for a ninety-day shutdown. I found myself struggling to think it was okay to put all that burden on production to build ahead, then manage it so there were no quality defects, and build the right number of parts since there was no way to build more once we tore the machines apart.

I tried to share the assembly way with powertrain leadership, but they could not even grasp the concept. They had not done weekend work as confirmation that Monday morning would start up just fine. My final chance to get at it was when the North America (NA) leadership had put an assembly director whom I had known previously in charge of powertrain. We prepared our typical approach as requested but separately developed an assembly-type approach that I put behind the typical presentation. As I imagined, the assembly experienced NA leader asked, "Why do we need such a long shutdown when they do model changes in nine days in assembly?"

After the hesitation to answer by powertrain leadership, I noted that I had been working on an idea that could get us to a nine-day shutdown but would require more weekend work, to which he replied, "Let's try it." Suddenly, getting at it meant move forward with confidence by breaking things down and organizing the work. It was paying off again. We were able to reveal our idea to the NA leadership and said we would get started. By not being afraid or getting analysis paralysis by wondering, "Is it okay to make an alternate plan?" our team showed our "Get at it" attitude and revolutionized model changes for powertrain by being confident and making a plan.

As one could imagine, no plan is perfect from the get-go. As we tore down those initial machines and tried to get them running for Monday, we soon learned there were some worn-out parts that had been compensated for but not well-documented. As we chose to keep getting at it, we had to add steps to confirm existing machine conditions and quality prior to teardown. We then had production get the existing parts back into specification to the original, or be willing to accept a deviation ahead of the work.

We realized we needed to have a hands-on member do the confirmations and even the more complex modifications as the equipment vendor technicians, who had traveled from Japan, were not readily available. To ensure we could get at it, I devised the strategy for the North American technicians, or *seibi*, as they are called in Japan. A year later, we launched a model change using a typical nine-day shutdown, which was the first time in the world for Toyota powertrain. Thanks, Dad, for we got at it.

Life lesson: By getting at it, we can use our previous experiences to improve new ones.

As I moved to in-house logistics at Toyota, I realized the group had never gotten past the idea of cost reduction, and it truly needed to have an ideal logistic concept, which the group was founded upon. I chose to get at it by first sharing the basic gaps we saw in logistics, or "visualize the gap," as we say at Toyota. I then had the team formulate the countermeasures for the area and determine the potential savings. The listeners were surprised and wanted us to look at how to get funding to implement it, and we did. By staying the course, getting at it, and keeping at it, we finally became a real section with headcount and an operating budget. I was so happy, for it was a great team of talented folks who loved to get at it. That team soon showed how more logistics space would save money, and we did our first example of this at Indiana.

Next, we created a vision for in-house logistics and managed to get funding to help a start-up who was developing the Amazon-type delivery system we needed. We were showing that getting at it in logistics was paying off, for it impacted every vehicle with dollars-per-unit savings. We easily made the less-than-two-year payback that was required while being able to implement the latest process and technology. By getting at it, we gained not only more capital but also more manpower to do deeper studies to save money. The team was confident, willing to make mistakes but also staying the course and adjust.

As I reflect on this experience, in addition to confidence, communication, and collaboration, a person must be willing to embrace dealing with the gaps and figure out how to communicate. I embraced the idea of getting at it for my home life as well. When we bought our Gaines Way house, I knew we needed to replace the kitchen cabinets. Our new home was a modern Victorian that had forty-five-degree angles in the kitchen walls, and I had purchased new used cabinets from a kitchen remodel, so I had to make what I had work. As I began to measure spaces, I went down in our basement where the cabinets were stored to see what cabinets would work. Suddenly, it hit me—the basement below had the same shape as the kitchen, with the forty-five-degree angles, so by just trying to get at it, I found a way to quickly lay out all the kitchen space. Now, with the actual cabinets, I could show my wife what the kitchen would look like, and easily adjust things before actually installing them.

Over the years, those same "aha" moments have happened, where just by getting at it, I suddenly found a solution to what I had been pondering for days, weeks, or even months. That aha moment happened on Gaines Way too when I was building our new theater room. I was worried about how to mount the projector so people could wander in and out without blacking out the screen. I decided I needed to get at it by just simply mounting the camera in the back of the space where I had planned. Once mounted, I ran an extension cord to see the result, and then I realized that my screen image is upside down. I then found the manual to study how to invert the screen, and suddenly, my other answer for minimizing people interference came in those pages as well. The manual actually showed how to make the projector angle change with the image while inverting it. Within thirty minutes, I inverted the image but could walk in and sit down on the theater room furniture without any interference to the image.

Another aha moment came when I decided to move the half-bath door at Gaines so people in the kitchen would not be staring at the toilet in the bathroom. After I demolished the adjacent hall closet, I realized we had enough space not just for a vanity but also a shower. That led me to realize that the front office could now be a guest bedroom with the addition of a closet, and they could have their own bathroom. By getting at it to move a door, I had now officially gone from a three-bedroom house to four.

When I decided to add a thirty-six-by-fifty-four-foot barn to house a shop and a three-car garage at Gaines Way, I realized I needed to figure out a layout to submit with the building permit. To get at it, I first set a line to make sure a car parked in front of the barn was at least two feet away from the line of the car backing out of the house garage. As I then considered how I would use the barn, I realized the man door of the barn should be straight across from the man door of the house garage for quick access to the shop inside the barn. As I was getting at it, I recognized I could use our cistern as a datum initially for the X/Y axis of the layout, but as I stood back at the top of the driveway, I recognized the need to set an elevation too.

From my study of history at the Biltmore in Asheville, North Carolina, I learned how the architect worked with George Vanderbilt to set the elevation of the house based on the view of Mount Pisgah from the rear veranda using a platform to emulate the height. Suddenly, I realized that my first view of the house and barn would be from the top of the driveway while riding in from the driveway in a car. Based on that, I made a board to simulate the gutter line of the barn and mounted it so I could see it from the top of the driveway. By adjusting the board by line of sight so it matched the gutter line of the house, I could now get an elevation from cistern datum. With that elevation, I could confirm the slope from the barn to the existing driveway to make sure we maintained proper storm water drainage. By deciding to get at it with the layout of the barn and using some past lessons learned on architectural design and function, I was able to create a barn that truly looked like a natural extension of the house garages.

As we finished the theater room at Gaines Way, I realized we still had space for a mini suite or apartment in the basement. By deciding to get at it, and through my available cabinets from the original kitchen upstairs, I laid out and installed the kitchen with the simple assumption for a thirty-inch refrigerator. Another aha moment was having a Corian countertop left over from the new used kitchen cabinets we bought for upstairs, then realizing it had a built-in sink, which made it clear where the cabinets needed to be as far as location. This ultimately set the layout, which fit perfectly. With the kitchen in place, the ideal location would be for both a bathroom and a bedroom became obvious. I had no idea that a few years later, my first grandson would be making that mini suite his home for the first ten months of his life as his parents were waiting on their new home to be built. I feel so blessed that my getting at it, as well as my son-in-law's, led to a space my own kids could use while building their family's dream home and their own. It felt like Gaines Way was just for us, as we built our family. My dad's words, "Get at it," were not only making a difference for me but also my family. Thanks, Dad.

As I started this chapter on "Getting at It," I noted how it was intentional to be the last life lesson. For as I have realized in my life, a word or thought without action is just another word or thought. As an engineer, we always talk about creating a plan, which consists of expectations, like constructing a building and planning the activities to meet those expectations, like digging the footers that ultimately support the building.

> **Life lesson: The thing I've realized is that the best-made plans are absolutely nothing without taking action.**

In addition, that action has be to be intentional. Intentional is the idea of being "quick as possible" and "as soon as possible." It is this "quick and soon as possible" focus that see so many people leave their dreams behind in ashes of "I wish I would have" or "I wish I could have" done something.

The "Get at it" mentality fixes the "I wish I would have" mentality by driving you to want to try and just see what happens. It is no different than deciding to write down *No Regrets* in 2011, not having a clue I would actually write a book about my dad's lessons to me. At the time I started, I only knew Dad's words and their impact on me when writing the start of that first chapter. It wasn't until 2016 and 2017, as I was turning fifty, that I realized I wanted to leave a legacy and found myself writing a eulogy about myself (which I'm attaching here as an appendix) to "begin or maybe continue with the end in mind," as Stephen Covey would say. Just by deciding to get at it and write my ideal life story did I realize how *No Regrets* could fit in as a legacy. With the idea of *No Regrets* becoming a way to live life by starting as a book, did I now have my antenna up to watch and learn how to write a book?

The rest of the answer would come in 2022 as I talked with Alinka Rutkowska of Leaders Press, who simply said, "Do you need help to outsource your book?" Alinka and the Leaders Press team have helped me finish "Getting at it" and *No Regrets*. Suddenly, like seeing red cars everywhere once you buy one, I now realize that to go get at it is paying attention to opportunities to make things happen by taking action. I'm so honored to have Leaders Press help me write *No Regrets* and just see what happens. My dad's words have helped me to push back the fears of the unknown.

The "Get at it" mentality fixes the "I wish I could have" by driving us to start. My dad was living proof of this as we built bathrooms, carports, kitchen additions, and so on. My dad's "Get at it" logic is well stated in the quote, "Don't let what you don't know disturb what you do know." As I shared earlier about getting started on work and home projects, I constantly discover the answers to the next steps along the way that may even originally had me hesitating to start in the first place. As I discover the answers, like as I shared on the theater room projector, I stop, laugh, and hear those words, "Get at It," for that's the way to do all I can.

Another way I discover ways to get at it is to ask the question, "What would you do if you did know the answer?" It's funny that it results in making clear what I do know, which lets me jump into action, and then the aha moment comes later, when I realize that here was the answer all along. I'm amazed how many times a day

I see people and their projects get stuck because they either don't know something or don't have something. At those moments, I find myself asking them ask why and then helping them realize there are other things they can do in the meantime, such as parallel work activities. There are other ways they can get something to work, such as using substitute materials from other vendors and other locations. I even use the "Begin with the end in mind" type of questions to help them reimagine the ideal expectation or situation, then inquire more with, "If you had no restraints, like people, time, or money, then what would you do?" It is then that I break down the ideal activities to help them find the way to get at it by finding ways to the necessary resources.

By using this approach, I believe people find ways to do things that look to be impossible, but as I have heard quoted from a great friend, Gary Dubuque, "The only difference between possible and impossible is time and money"—the time to figure things out and the money to get the necessary people and resources to put it all together. As I look back on life with my dad, I never heard him say the word "impossible," and I realize it's because of his "Get at it" combined with his "You can do anything if you put your mind to it." These beliefs truly he made all things possible. It's this same mindset that I use to approach all the projects in my life.

My "Get at it" in life has led to my twenty-eight years of capital projects in most of our eighty-two sites of manufacturing, logistics, sales, and parts with spending in the billions and with the help of hundreds of team members and contractors who also have become great friends. Those "Get at it" moments helped me make sure over thirty-two thousand team members had new work or more work to do due to the new equipment and spaces that the team helped me to create.

I wonder if my dad realized how much his "Get at it" attitude would impact others. As I ponder that, I realize he probably did. That attitude led to a house being finished that I grew up in, our neighbors' and friends' broken cars being fixed, a kitchen addition for Grandma Lestie, and dozens of homes around the Dayton, Ohio, area being painted or remodeled to make way for a renewed life. I recall my aunts, uncles, cousins, and friends talking about my dad's willingness to get at it and how his work ethic never wavered.

I believe we are innately built to get at it for that higher power made us in his image to be cocreators. I believe he hopes that someday we can all align our "Get at it" in order to help each other. I believe he hopes that my sharing of my dad's words will inspire others to do likewise, and in the end, it could erase the idea of hunger and homelessness. Imagine "We the people" all being "Get at it" type of people, where engineers could create unique mobility equipment that handicapped people would want to use in their desire to contribute. Cooks would prepare meals for the hungry so they could contribute better. Farmers would grow crops for food so that cooks could feed the hungry. We can then imagine that people ready to get at it would drive or motivate others to get at it too, leading to a much better world.

I hope now that those who knew "Don't ever say you're waiting on something in front of Casel" now understand why. It was not about having an excuse, but all about my belief and understanding of "Get at it." I know this attitude of will allow anyone to find a way to get started even while working on a countermeasure for the issue that would have left you waiting. I know that many times the answer gets discovered as you're working on something that is right next to it. I want people to "not wait" as well, for the one thing we cannot replace is time.

Life lesson: Not waiting for the whole or perfect answer and taking action are keys to go get at it.

In the end, I believe moving forward shows our faith in the higher power that something will happen. It's why I have found out that I discover the missing answers as I move forward with the answers I know.

Thanks, Dad!

CLOSING THOUGHTS ON THE JOURNEY

Since I shared in the introduction how *No Regrets* came to be, I wanted to share further about my journey and conviction for the need to share this story.

As you have learned by now, these ten sayings that my dad used were translated into real-life definitions and stories of my own. As I finish sharing these stories about how my dad's words made a difference in my life, I have been humbled by his words being somewhat silenced by his recent physical condition of Alzheimer's and dementia.

It's now a treat to hear him suddenly recall lines like, "You know, a person can do anything if you put your mind to it." He then shared his commitment to his dad's use of a check row corn planter back in high school. His dad had asked him, "Do you think you can figure this thing out?" and all my dad said was, "I think so," which led to him planting ten acres of corn in perfect rows. As an engineer, I had to look up a what check row planter was and realized that this was so important to allow a farmer to have perfectly spaced plants so they could periodically weed the corn by plowing, since this was before the days of chemical weed control.

I share my dad's condition to make you realize that someday, all of our words will be silenced, whether by a disease as my dad has, or at the very least, the end of this life as we know it. As a person who now understands this reality of "silence" and the human desire to leave a legacy, it makes the utmost sense to do to our very best to look back on our life with *No Regrets*.

No Regrets applies to our thinking, choices, actions, impact, and what we leave behind.

No Regrets only comes from being our best in the moment, adjusting, apologizing, and then carrying on with a new vigor to get better.

No Regrets comes as well from our sharing of life experiences in the hope that someone else may have a simpler path and possibly a better or further result.

I thank my dad and all those who shared their life with me to help me, make me better, and "sharpen my saw" at all times, especially the tough ones.

I thank you and all the future readers for allowing me to share that I have *no regrets* for what I have done, failed to do, and have yet to do, for at least I have shared my life lessons in the hope that you all may have a simpler path or, at the very best, a much better destination.

CASEL'S BIBLE (CREATED 2002)

Here are notes from the coach's desk and words to live by:

- Don't let what you don't know disturb what you do know.
- Don't get the paralysis of analysis. Just do something.
- What's a plan? Expectations and activities to meet them.
- LTD or "Living the dream"
- Remember when Thomas Edison was asked, "Why didn't you give up after ten thousand failures of the light bulb?" he replied, "For after finding all the wrong ways, there is only one thing left—the right way!"
- Dream, believe, dare, do.
- When faced with a decision, consider this from Dr. Robert Schuller: "What would you attempt if you knew you could not fail?"
- There are four basic human needs: to live, to love, to Learn, and to leave a legacy. Start now!

Here are words from the great inventor and builder Charles F. Kettering as well:

> Nothing ever built arose to touch the skies
> Unless one man willed that it should,
> Unless one man willed that it must.

Your life story is what you make it. Mine started with a visit to Abraham Lincoln's birthplace with my parents. There I learned the great lessons in life at nine years old: hard work, perseverance, and integrity in the moment of choice.

A EULOGY FOR CASEL BURNETT (12/5/2016)

I "pre-wrote" this eulogy as a way to describe what I hope will be my legacy—what I want to leave to my kids, my grandkids, and my community.

The Day the World Came to Know "Flyte"
A Great Father and a Contributor to Society Has Passed

Casel Burnett of Walton, KY, passed today from natural causes. He was the cofounder of LODI that has led the way in cutting-edge technology development for children and the aging.

Mr. Burnett codeveloped the "Flyte" automated growing rod that revolutionized medicine, allowing children to have a normal life while living with and growing out of scoliosis. This device has allowed thousands of children to receive the needed support for their spine with the aid of an internal device that sends necessary information to their physician, which, in turn, allows them to make complex, multiplane adjustments as needed and as often as seen fit. This has children leaving adolescence with a straight spine, for it was later integrated with the muscular system therapy called "Wings" that enhances and ensures the necessary muscle control to hold the spine straight on its own.

Mr. Burnett codeveloped the "Waltonian" community with his daughter Ashley, who is the chairman and the director of health with a master's degree in nursing. The Waltonian has become a family legacy with his wife, Michele, who is a board director and the director of hospitality; his daughter Amanda, who is CEO and the director of external affairs; his son Blake, who is the vice president and director of marketing/sales; his son Landon, who is the president and director of research and development; his son-in-law Douglas Patton, who is the director of safety and security; and his grandson Brayden Patton who is the regional manager of the Eastern Region.

The Waltonian is known for its Disney approach to community, where young and old cohabitate to support each other physically, mentally, emotionally, technically, and spiritually. The Burnetts have created an approach that many have tried to mimic, but can only be found successful in the grateful members and benefactors of the Waltonian community. It's the only example where community and industry are seamlessly integrated so that people and technology combine for the ultimate life experience.

Mr. Burnett's love for the automobile never wavered throughout his life. His father, William, instilled that love at a young age, which led to an amazing automotive career, starting at General Motors in Dayton, Ohio, and spreading across the entire North and Central American continents, with his executive roles at Toyota Motors North America in production engineering. Prior to finishing up his working career at Toyota, Mr. Burnett created the "people" culture of innovation at their headquarters office in Georgetown, KY, which is now a destination for families of future engineers/inventors/entrepreneurs, where the production engineering organization provides camps for kids in addition to lab space to support their development.

Mr. Burnett developed NKU's "Imagineering School" in partnership with Disney and a local high-school academy that now is responsible for the development of STEAM curriculum for the entire country. Mr. Burnett's passion for innovation and implementation is a testimony to his work ethic and vision of an ever-better future for all, which is the foundational thinking of the schools.

Mr. Burnett and his wife, Michele, codeveloped LODI, starting with their real estate investment management, which provided the foundation to establish the Waltonian community. LODI set the standards for landlord/tenant relationships across the globe and has led to a property management and project management empire with employees around the globe who provide Disney-like service to tenants and landlord clients.

Mr. Burnett has clearly passed on his passion in work ethic and innovation not only to his family but also to the thousands of employees and clients of his well-established companies. His autobiography, *No Regrets*, well summarizes what drove him through his entire life. *No Regrets* has now become a following of its own and is even offered in the STEAM curriculum across the USA as part of the "Innovate and Implement" classes.

Mr. Burnett and his wife, Michele, established the Burnett Foundation, which now provides millions a year in financial support to spread the No Regrets philosophy to children and adults in need.

Mr. Burnett wanted the world to know his father's greatest lesson ("You can do anything if you put your mind to it") and that his wife was his reason to carry on in the face of adversity. Mr. Burnett fell in love with his beautiful blue-eyed lady while in high school and stayed mesmerized by the lady he called his "pretty blues" all the rest of his days.

Mr. Burnett and his family wish to thank all those who walked with them and helped them on the journey of Casel's life. Mr. Burnett will have a celebration of his life at the NKU Center, where donations can be made to the Burnett Foundation in lieu of flowers/gifts.

Mr. Burnett asked us to let all who knew him know that he is still "living the dream" with his Heavenly Father now, and is smiling down at this moment as you reminisce about the time you spent with him.

All the Best,
Casel Burnett

ACKNOWLEDGMENTS

To my parents, I would like to thank them for their great examples of hard work and perseverance, which comes from growing up as farmers in Appalachia where hard work is a given. These values are the ones that allowed me to "get at it" and kept me going even when the work called for all-nighters to ensure start-ups would happen in the morning.

To my family, I would like to thank them for allowing me countless hours of being away in manufacturing plants around North America installing new processes and equipment for construction of new models of vehicles. These experiences allowed me to learn, grow, and become a leader which could only come from "being in the field."

To my first great mentor and engineering teacher, Dennis Desilets, who called me "grasshopper." It was Dennis who showed me "how to take what was in the real-world" and figure out "how to simulate things from an engineering perspective" so that I could build ever-better equipment and processes. I was able to seek him out and thank him before he passed away, which I am so thankful for being able to do so. I'm sure God is using Dennis abilities to make heaven an even better place.

To a great friend, David Fernandes, who encouraged me, saying "Casel Burnett, you should write a book," when

I shared my thoughts and life lessons on leadership as we discussed our struggles as executives at the time.

To my Toyota family, who allowed me to make countless mistakes as I worked alongside the greatest engineering, production, and trades people in North America. I am honored by all those who helped me and followed me through some very challenging moments as we prepared great vehicles for our customers.

To my Leaders Press family, who have worked tirelessly to help me make my dream of leaving a legacy come alive in these pages, and to Alinka Rutkowska for reaching out and asking me, "Casel, have you ever thought of writing a book?" I knew at that moment that Leaders Press was where I was supposed to become an author.

ABOUT CASEL BURNETT

Casel Burnett, a distinguished construction leader in the automotive industry, leverages his vast experience to inspire and enable others to harness their potential. His entrepreneurial ventures and the establishment of his own companies underscore the pivotal role that life lessons from others played in his success.

Casel received degrees in mechanical engineering and manufacturing management from the University of Dayton and Kettering University. In his professional activities, he has combined management talent and hands-on technical expertise to streamline operations, increase productivity, and reduce costs, driving bottom-line improvement at Toyota and General Motors. Highly skilled in troubleshooting and solving problems, he has improved operations by leading teams to achieve efficiencies through innovative procedures and processes.

Casel directed major capital projects to on-schedule completion at Toyota, where he rose through the ranks to the executive level, becoming group manager of production engineering. In this role, he implemented $280M in annual capital projects for NA-wide building expansions/modifications/utilities. Also at Toyota, he implemented standardization of an NA-wide in-house logistics process with $360M in annual operations. He implemented a repair parts strategy to eliminate a 7 percent annual inventory growth, saving $17M annually. He also implemented a new Toyota production strategy and plan, cutting shutdown time by 82 percent and costs by $26.5M. Additionally, he led an engineering team to identify cost-cutting initiatives, producing $3M in capital project savings.

Throughout his career, Casel has demonstrated skill in implementing continuous process improvements and building, training, and coaching high-performance operations and production teams. He seeks to act as a catalyst for and lead change throughout an organization. He strives to simplify complex processes in order to get things done quickly in ever-changing environments.

His mission is to build a foundation from the publication of his book, *No Regrets: What My Dad Tried to Teach Me and I Now Know*, that will support his vision of sharing one of his father's greatest lessons of "You can do anything if you put your mind to it" to help children and adults "innovate and implement" to make our world an even better place.

Casel is a member of the Project Management Professionals (PMP) and an engineering technology adjunct faculty member at Northern Kentucky University. He is also a member of the Ohio Automotive Industry Council (Ohio State University) manufacturing operations and a member of an industry group to ensure automotive manufacturing competitiveness in the state of Ohio. He served on the business development board of the Northern Kentucky Education Council – Action Team 5. He is a member of the advisory board of the Northern Kentucky University engineering technology program.